THE DIVINE COMEDY

INFERNO

THE DIVINE COMEDY
INFERNO

Dante

Supplementary material written by Frederic Will

Series edited by Cynthia Brantley Johnson

POCKET BOOKS
NEW YORK LONDON TORONTO SYDNEY

This book is a work of fiction. Names, characters, places and incidents are products of the author's imagination or are used fictitiously. Any resemblance to actual events or locales or persons, living or dead, is entirely coincidental.

POCKET BOOKS, a division of Simon & Schuster, Inc.
1230 Avenue of the Americas, New York, NY 10020

Supplementary materials copyright © 2005 by Simon & Schuster, Inc.

ISBN 13: 978-1-4165-0023-0
ISBN 10:   1-4165-0023-5

First Pocket Books printing May 2005

10 9 8 7 6 5 4 3

POCKET and colophon are registered trademarks of
Simon & Schuster, Inc.

Cover art by Marco Ventura

Manufactured in the United States of America

For information regarding special discounts for bulk purchases,
please contact Simon & Schuster Special Sales at 1-800-456-6798
or business@simonandschuster.com

CONTENTS

The Inferno:
GIVING THE WORLD HELL

At the beginning of the *Inferno,* we are introduced to a man who could well be our contemporary. In the middle of his life he is lost, conflicted about the direction he should take, and menaced by opponents. A lion, a she-wolf, and a leopard confront him, and he is nearly done for when suddenly a figure appears. It is the Roman poet Virgil, who will be his guide through the dark landscape which lies ahead of him: a voyage through Hell.

The *Inferno,* completed in 1314, is only the first third of Dante's great work, *The Divine Comedy.* In the second and third sections, Dante voyages through Purgatory, and finally to Paradise. While for many readers Dante's first journey is the most interesting, it is useful to remember that in Dante's time the blessings of paradise were the sole justification for Dante's intrepid travels. The three-part structure of *The Divine Comedy* was crucial to Dante's authorial vision, and the focus on the number three, which has great significance in Christian theology, extended into the smallest details of the work. While this translation is rendered as a prose narrative, the original work is an epic poem, employing a *terza rima* verse structure. Each stanza of the poem consists of three lines, the first and third of which rhyme together, while the middle line rhymes with the first and third lines of the following three-line stanza. Each book of *The Divine Comedy*—*Inferno*, *Purgatorio*, *Paradiso*—consists of thirty-three roughly coequal cantos which, added together, total ninety-nine cantos. Add the one introductory canto, you have a total of one hundred. This number, ten times itself, was considered "perfect" in medieval mystical thought. The entire poem, therefore, can be seen as an elaborately wrought divine puzzle and an intricately worked prayer to God.

European and American critics of the past century have consistently praised the literary value and lasting human importance of *The Divine Comedy*. However, Dante's *Commedia* has not always been widely admired. The great German poet Goethe, for example, wasn't sure what to think. At one point (in Rome, July 1787) he says, "I found the *Inferno* monstrous, the *Purgatorio* ambiguous, and the *Paradiso* boring." In Italy, the work was virtually forgotten during the nineteenth century, while in European literary circles of the time the *Inferno* was found too coarse, violent, and medieval. It was not until a famous twentieth-century American poet, T. S. Eliot, published his own master work, *The Waste Land* (1922), that appreciation for Dante's work was rekindled. *The Waste Land*, a modernist poetic masterpiece that examines the "hell" following World War One, bears several similarities to

Dante's *Inferno,* and Eliot, an influential champion of Dante, alludes to *The Divine Comedy* several times in his work. Eliot showed cynical modern readers that the shades, the sinners, and the tormented inhabitants of *The Waste Land* are the direct descendants of the citizens of Dante's Hell—and the brothers and sisters of us all.

The Life and Work of Dante Alighieri

Dante Alighieri was born in Florence in the last days of 1265. For parallels to the vitality of that environment we would need to go back to ancient Athens, with its bubblingly vital city-state culture of the fifth century B.C. Mid–thirteenth-century Florence was exploding with political fervor, economic drive, and artistic creativity. Many citizens participated actively in their local government. At the same time, serious rifts appeared in the politics of the city, and the instability of the resulting clashes left many people endangered by swift changes in the political winds—Dante himself was exiled in 1302. But it also sparked a brilliance that contributed lasting beauty and understanding to the growth of modern culture.

Born into a family of medium wealth and recent nobility, Dante seems to have enjoyed a happy enough childhood, with two sisters and a brother. He was carefully educated by both the Dominicans and the Franciscans, two monastic orders founded in the early thirteenth century, famous for the high-quality teaching their monks provided. Dante read widely from youth on, focusing especially on Italian and Provençal

poets. His "first friend" was the poet Guido Caval-
canti, but he was only the first, for Dante plunged vig-
orously into the vital creative and cultural life of
Florence. More than a few of the figures we meet in
the *Inferno* were from Dante's immediate circle. He
married about 1285, and had two sons and (it has been
conjectured) two daughters. In 1289 he took part in
his first military campaign, and in 1295 he began to
participate actively in city politics. He was involved in
governance, in street supervision, and more broadly in
resisting those projects of the papacy that infringed on
Florentine sovereignty. It was in connection with the
latter efforts that Dante, on a mission to Rome, found
himself condemned, on trumped-up charges, to ban-
ishment and fine, and ultimately to death by burning.
From that time on, Dante did not return to Florence.
We know only episodes from the last twenty years of
his life in banishment, but come away with a picture
of ebbing political hopes, close friendships with pa-
trons, and, beyond that, a difficult, intellectually rest-
less life of exile.

Of Dante's life and work, the last thing—the most
important thing—to be mentioned is Beatrice, his
muse. Dante first saw Beatrice when he was nine and
she was eight. Though she would become of utmost im-
portance to his work, he glimpsed her only occasionally
from then on up to her death in 1290. Beatrice was
real, but also ideal, from the start. Dante identified
Beatrice's name and form with the supreme grace of
the Virgin Mary, which ultimately calls him to Paradise.
Beatrice sheds her influence over the whole *Comme-
dia*, interceding for him in Hell, and sparing and guid-

ing him as he rises through Purgatory to the blinding light of Heaven.

Historical and Literary Context of the *Inferno* and *The Divine Comedy*

Political Turmoil: Florence, the Papacy, and the Empire

Dante's life and city were part of a vastly complex and rapidly changing medieval world of new commerce, proto–nation-states, stretching global frontiers, and new technologies for warfare and labor. The world-political struggle looming around the rapidly developing city of Florence was basically a struggle between the emperors of the Holy Roman Empire and the Papacy. Politics within the city of Florence largely concerned attitudes toward these two major power blocs. In 1266, when Dante was only a few months old, the Church and its Guelf party (the party of the Papacy) won a major battle against the imperialist Ghibellines at the Battle of Benevento. The rulers of the new mercantile cultural Florence were ardent supporters of the Guelf party yet at the same time eager to maintain their independence from the Papacy (no small balancing act, and a political tightrope along which Dante tried to walk).

The historical setting of Dante's Florence would have been sufficiently complex as just described. But the Empire-Papacy split did not allow for easy allegiances, and within the Guelf party, in Florence, there were two factions, the established, aristocratic Blacks and the newly arrived, mercantile Whites. The Whites, the party to which Dante belonged, were determined to maintain a working balance between Papacy and Empire. The Blacks, on the other hand, were willing to deal with the Church to maintain their own advantage. The exile of Dante, the determinant fact of his spiritual life, derived from his advocacy of the White party.

All of these struggles impinged concretely on Dante's life and work. The *Inferno* is littered with victims of political corruption, fraudulent manipulation, overcivilized vice—and with the moral fortitude of Aeneas, Beatrice, Cato, and the author, figures of ascent and faith. Dante had many temperaments, but he was always a realist. He wrote from his experience of a world in which the greatest secular and religious powers he believed in were fighting one another for both his pocketbook and his soul.

Classical Roman Literature and the Beginnings of Vernacular Literature

To understand the miracle of Dante's artistic achievement, we need to appreciate the matrix from which it was born. Two centuries before Dante began to write, literature in the West was recorded in Latin and based on Roman culture and history. Foremost among the Roman poets, for Dante, was Virgil, whom Dante made his guide through Hell in the *Inferno*. In the *Aeneid* (19 B.C.), which Dante knew by heart, Virgil describes the aftermath of the great Trojan War. Under the leadership of Aeneas, the defeated Trojans sail to Latium, in southern Italy, and found what is to become the Roman Empire, thus to be considered the direct ancestors of

the Italians. Dante revered Virgil for having grasped
the seminal importance of Aeneas, the hero of the
Aeneid, for both the Roman Empire and the Papacy—
the two sustaining pillars of Dante's own world—were
made possible by the voyage of the Trojans as described
in Virgil's epic poem.

Not long after the end of the first millennium, a
new, more popular, more localized literature began to
emerge from under the shadow of this heritage. Its
languages were the forerunners of modern Italian,
French, and Spanish—the vernacular—as opposed to
Latin, which remained the formal language of law and
the Church. This is the literature that forged the tradi-
tion of which Dante's work would be part. In both
France and Italy courtly poetry was being produced
by troubadours, while longer texts were being created
by writers of romance. (The *Romance of the Rose*,
completed about 1274, was a powerful example of the
new imagination.) This literature was fueled by the
burst of creative intellectual life then under way. The
new universities of France and especially of Italy were
making themselves centers of creativity in the arts as
well as in science and theology. Meanwhile, the im-
mensely influential texts of Aristotle were being re-
leased into the mainstream of Western culture in a
series of important translations, and thinkers and spir-
itualists like Saint Francis of Assisi and Saint Thomas
Aquinas were inspiring radical new perspectives on
human existence.

To all of these new movements Dante was a lively
heir, as were his successors Petrarch and Boccaccio,
who drove forward the powerful engine of modern Ital-

ian literature. Petrarch (1304–74) brought the sonnet to a new peak, while Boccaccio (1313–75) created, in his ribald *Decameron,* what might be considered the first novel. But it was Dante who truly opened up the new Italian language and made it available to both of these brilliant successors.

CHRONOLOGY OF DANTE'S LIFE AND WORK

1265: Dante Alighieri born.

1277: Begins study of Latin. He is promised in marriage to Gemma Donati.

1283: Writes his first lyrics after his first encounter with ideal true love, Beatrice.

1285: Marries Gemma Donati.

1287: First child. Dante participates in military campaigns.

1290: Beatrice dies.

1292: Dante finishes writing the *Vita Nuova*, a lyrical work about his love for Beatrice.

1300: Corso Donati, the main figure of the Black Guelfs, is banished. Dante is elected one of six priors (governors) of Florence.

1301: Dante thought to have been on mission to Pope Boniface VIII.

1302: Dante's allegiance to the Whites becomes perilous, as that party is banished from Florence. He is condemned to exile by the Black priorate.

1303: Dante lingers in Tuscany, hoping to return to Florence.

1304: Composes the *Convivio,* a philosophical work.

1307: Visits Paris. Begins work on *The Divine Comedy.*

1311: Completes *De Monarchia,* a treatise on government, and *De Vulgari Eloquentia,* defending the use of vernacular languages for serious writings.

1312: Meets Emperor Henry VII.

1313: Completes the *Inferno.*

1321: Dante is guest of Can Grande della Scala at Verona.

1317–1321: Resides at Ravenna under patronage of the Count of Polenta.

1321: Dies of malaria in Ravenna.

HISTORICAL CONTEXT OF
Inferno

1215: Guelfs and Ghibellines, warring political factions in Florence, begin a power struggle for control of the city that spans two generations.

1273: Thomas Aquinas completes *Summa Theologica*.

1274: Edward I crowned king of England at Westminster.

1277: Roger Bacon imprisoned for heresy.

1280: Kublai Khan founds Yuan Dynasty in China.

1281: Pope Martin IV ascends to the Vatican Papacy.

1282: In the Sicilian Vespers, the Sicilians rebel against French domination of Sicily, and most of the French on the island are massacred.

1284: Genoa defeats Pisa at the Battle of Meloria, initiating its decline.

1288: Osman I founds Ottoman Empire.

1291: Mamelukes conquer Acre, ending Christian rule in the East.

1294: Kublai Khan dies.

1296: Frederick II becomes king of Sicily.

1297: Genoese defeat Venetians in major sea battle.

1299: Treaties are made between Venice and the Turks.

1300: Pope Boniface VIII announces Jubilee Year.

1301: Boniface sends Charles of Valois and his army to quash anti-Church forces in Florence.

1302: First meeting held of French states-general.

1306: Robert Bruce crowned king of Scots.

1308: Edward II crowned king of England.

1312: Henry VII crowned Holy Roman Emperor.

1313: Henry VII dies.

1316: Edward Bruce crowned king of Ireland.

1320: Peace of Paris established between Flanders and France.

1322: Battle of Muehldorf fought; Frederick of Austria defeated and taken prisoner by Louis of Bavaria.

1325: Aztecs found their capital, Tenochtitlán. It will become Mexico City after the Spanish conquest and subsequent independence of Mexico.

1326: Osman I, ruler of Turkey, dies.

1327: Edward II, deposed by English parliament, succeeded by Edward III.

THE DIVINE COMEDY

INFERNO

CANTO I

Dante, astray in a wood, reaches the foot of a hill which he begins to ascend; he is hindered by three beasts; he turns back and is met by Virgil, who proposes to guide him into the eternal world.

M IDWAY UPON THE JOURNEY OF OUR LIFE[1] I found myself in a dark wood, where the right way was lost. Ah! how hard a thing it is to tell what this wild and rough and difficult wood was, which in thought renews my fear! So bitter is it that death is little more. But in order to treat of the good that I found in it, I will tell of the other things that I saw there.

I cannot well report how I entered it, so full was I of slumber at that moment when I abandoned the true way. But after I had reached the foot of a hill, where that valley ended which had pierced my heart with fear, I looked upward, and saw its shoulders clothed already with the rays of the planet which leads man aright along every path. Then was the fear a little quieted which had lasted in the lake of my heart through the night that I had passed so piteously. And even as one who with spent breath, issued forth from the sea upon the shore, turns to the perilous water and gazes, so did my mind, which still was flying, turn back to look again upon the pass which never left person alive.

After I had rested a little my weary body, I again took my way along the desert slope, so that the firm foot was always the lower. And lo! almost at the beginning of the steep a she-leopard,[2] light and very nimble, which was covered with a spotted coat. And she did not withdraw from before my face, nay, hindered so my road that I often turned to go back.

The time was the beginning of the morning, and the Sun was mounting up with those stars that were with him when the Love Divine first set in motion those beautiful things; so that the hour of the time and the sweet season were occasion to me of good hope concerning that wild beast with the dappled skin; but not so that the sight which appeared to me of a lion[3] did not give me fear. He appeared to be coming against me, with his head high and with ravening hunger, so that it appeared that the air was affrighted at him; and a she-wolf, which in her leanness seemed laden with all cravings, and ere now had made many folk to live forlorn,—she brought on me so much heaviness, with the fear that came from sight of her, that I lost hope of the height. And such as is he who gains willingly, and the time arrives which makes him lose, so that in all his thoughts he laments and is sad, such did the beast without peace make me, which, coming on against me, was pushing me back, little by little, thither where the Sun is silent.

While I was falling back to the low place, one who appeared faint-voiced through long silence presented himself before my eyes. When I saw him in the great desert, "Have pity on me!" I cried to him, "whatso thou be, whether shade or real man." He answered me: "Not man; man once I was, and my parents were Lombards, and both Mantuans by country. I was born *sub Julio*, though late, and I lived at Rome under the good Augustus, at the time of the false and lying gods. I was a poet, and sang of that just son of Anchises who came from Troy, after proud Ilion had been burned. But thou, why dost thou return to such great annoy? Why dost thou not ascend the delectable mountain which is the source and cause of all joy?" "Art thou then that Virgil[4] and that fount which pours forth so broad a stream of speech?" replied I with bashful front to him: "O honor and light of the other poets! may the long study avail me and the great love, which have made me search thy volume! Thou art my master and my author; thou alone art he from whom I took the fair style that has done me honor. Behold the beast because of which I turned; help me against her, famous sage, for she makes my veins and pulses tremble." "It behoves thee to hold another course," he replied, when he saw me weeping, "if thou wouldst escape from this savage place; for this beast, because of which thou criest out, lets not any one pass along her way, but so hinders him that she kills him; and she has a nature so malign and evil that she never sates her greedy will, and after food has more hunger than before. Many are the animals with which she wives, and there shall be more yet, until the hound shall come that will make her die of grief. He shall not feed on land or pelf, but wisdom and love and valor, and his birthplace shall be between Feltro and Feltro. Of that low Italy shall he be the salvation, for which the virgin Camilla died, and Euryalus, Turnus and Nisus of their wounds. He shall hunt her through every town till he shall have put her back again in Hell, there whence envy first sent her forth. Wherefore I think and deem it for thy best that thou follow me, and I will be thy guide, and will lead thee hence through the eternal place where thou shalt hear the despairing shrieks, shalt see the ancient spirits woeful who each proclaim the second death. And then thou shalt see those who are contented in the fire, because they hope to come, whenever it may be, to the blessed folk; to whom if thou wouldst then ascend, there shall be a soul[5] more worthy than I for that. With her I will leave thee at my departure; for that Emperor who reigns thereabove wills not, because I was rebellious to His law, that through me any one should come into His city. In all parts He governs and there He reigns: there is His city and His lofty seat. O happy the man whom thereto He elects!" And I to him: "Poet, I beseech thee by that God whom thou didst not know, in order that I may escape this ill and worse, that thou lead me thither where thou now hast said, so that I may see the gate of St. Peter,[6] and those whom thou reportest so afflicted."

Then he moved on, and I held behind him.

CANTO II

Dante, doubtful of his own powers, is discouraged at the outset.—Virgil cheers him by telling him that he has been sent to his aid by a blessed Spirit from Heaven, who revealed herself as Beatrice.— Dante casts off fear, and the poets proceed.

THE DAY WAS GOING, and the dusky air was taking the living things that are on earth from their fatigues, and I alone was preparing to sustain the war alike of the journey and of the woe, which my memory that errs not shall retrace.

O Muses,[1] O lofty genius, now assist me! O memory that didst inscribe that which I saw, here shall thy nobility appear!

I began:—

"Poet, who guidest me, consider my power, if it be sufficient, before thou trust me to the deep pass. Thou

sayest that the parent of Silvius while still corruptible
went to the immortal world and was there in the body;
and truly if the Adversary of every ill was courteous to
him, it seems not unmeet to the man of understanding,
thinking on the high effect that should proceed from
him, and on the who and the what; for in the empyrean
heaven he was chosen for father of revered Rome and
of her empire; both which (would one say truth) were
ordained for the holy place where the successor of the
greater Peter has his seat. Through this going, whereof
thou givest him vaunt, he learned things which were
the cause of his victory and of the papal mantle. After-
ward the Chosen Vessel[2] went thither to bring thence
comfort to that faith which is the beginning of the way
of salvation. But I, why go I thither? or who concedes
it? I am not Aeneas, I am not Paul; neither I nor others
believe me worthy of this; wherefore if I yield myself to
go, I fear lest the going may be mad. Thou art wise,
thou understandest better than I speak."

And as is he who unwills what he willed, and by rea-
son of new thoughts changes his purpose, so that he
withdraws wholly from what he had begun, such I be-
came on that dark hillside: because in my thought I
abandoned the enterprise which had been so hasty in
its beginning.

"If I have rightly understood thy speech," replied
that shade of the magnanimous one, "thy soul is hurt by
cowardice, which oftentimes encumbers a man so that
it turns him back from honorable enterprise, as false
seeing does a beast when it shies. In order that thou
loose thee from this fear I will tell thee why I came, and
what I heard at the first moment that I grieved for thee.

I was among those who are suspended,[3] and a Lady blessed and beautiful called me, such that I besought her to command. Her eyes were more shining than the star, and she began to say to me sweet and clear, with angelic voice, in her speech: 'O courteous Mantuan soul! of whom the fame yet lasts in the world, and shall last so long as motion continues, my friend, and not of fortune, is so hindered on his road upon the desert hillside that he has turned for fear, and I am afraid, through that which I have heard of him in heaven, lest he be already so astray that I may have risen late to his succor. Now do thou move, and with thy ornate speech and with whatever is needful for his deliverance, assist him so that I may be consoled thereby. I am Beatrice who make thee go. I come from a place whither I desire to return. Love moved me, that makes me speak. When I shall be before my Lord, I will often praise thee to Him.' Then she was silent, and thereon I began: 'O Lady of Virtue! through whom alone the human race excels all contained within that heaven which has the smallest circles, thy command so pleases me that to obey it, were it already done, were slow to me. There is no need for thee further to open to me thy will; but tell me the reason why thou dost not beware of descending down here into this centre, from the ample place whither thou burnest to return.' 'Since thou wishest to know so inwardly, I will tell thee briefly,' she replied to me, 'wherefore I fear not to come here within. One need be afraid only of those things that have power to do one harm, of others not, for they are not fearful. I am made by God, thanks be to Him, such that your misery touches me not, nor does the flame of this burning assail me. A gentle Lady[4] is in heaven who feels compassion for this hindrance whereto I send thee, so that she breaks stern judgment there above. She summoned Lucia[5] in her request, and said, "Thy faithful one now has need of thee, and I commend him to thee." Lucia, the foe of every cruel one, moved and came to the place where I was, seated with the ancient Rachel.[6] She said, "Beatrice, true praise of God, why dost thou not succor him who so loved thee that for thee he came forth from the vulgar throng? Dost thou not hear the pity of his plaint? Dost thou not see the death that combats him on the stream where the sea has no vaunt?" Never were persons in the world swift to do their good, or to fly their harm, as I, after these words were uttered, came down here from my blessed seat, putting my trust in thy upright speech, which honors thee and them who have heard it.' After she had said this to me, weeping she turned her lucent eyes, whereby she made me more quick to come. And I came to thee thus as she willed. I withdrew thee from before that wild beast which took from thee the short way on the beautiful mountain. What is it then? Why, why dost thou hold back? why dost thou harbor such cowardice in thy heart? why hast thou not daring and assurance, since three such blessed Ladies care for thee in the court of Heaven, and my speech pledges thee such good?"

As the flowerets, bent and closed by the chill of night, when the sun brightens them erect themselves all open on their stem, so I became with my drooping courage, and such good daring ran to my heart that I began like a person enfreed: "O compassionate she who succored me, and courteous thou who didst speedily obey the true words that she addressed to thee! Thou by thy words hast so disposed my heart with desire of going, that I have returned to my first intent. Now go, for one sole will is in us both: thou leader, thou lord, and thou master." Thus I said to him; and when he moved on, I entered along the deep and savage road.

CANTO III

The gate of Hell.—Virgil leads Dante in.—The punishment of those who had lived without infamy and without praise.—Acheron, and the sinners on its bank.—Charon.—Earthquake.—Dante swoons.

THROUGH ME IS the way into the woeful city; through me is the way into the eternal woe; through me is the way among the lost people. Justice moved my lofty maker: the divine Power, the supreme Wisdom and the primal Love made me. Before me were no things created, save eternal, and I eternal last. Leave every hope, ye who enter!"

These words of obscure color I saw written at the top of a gate; whereat I: "Master, their meaning is dire to me."

And he to me, like a person well advised: "Here it

behoves to leave every fear; it behoves that all cowardice should here be dead. We have come to the place where I have told thee that thou shalt see the woeful people, who have lost the good of the understanding."

And when he had put his hand on mine with a cheerful look, wherefrom I took courage, he brought me within to the secret things. Here sighs, laments, and deep wailings were resounding through the starless air; wherefore at first I wept thereat. Strange tongues, horrible utterances, words of woe, accents of anger, voices high and faint, and sounds of hands with them, were making a tumult which whirls always in that air forever dark, like the sand when the whirlwind breathes.

And I, who had my head girt with horror, said: "Master, what is that which I hear? and what folk is it that seems so overcome with its woe?"

And he to me: "The wretched souls of those who lived without infamy and without praise maintain this miserable mode. They are mingled with that caitiff choir of the angels, who were not rebels, nor were faithful to God, but were for themselves. The heavens chased them out in order to be not less beautiful, nor does the deep Hell receive them, for the damned would have some boast of them."

And I: "Master, what is so grievous to them, that makes them lament so bitterly?"

He answered: "I will tell thee very briefly. These have not hope of death; and their blind life is so debased, that they are envious of every other lot. Fame of them the world permits not to be; mercy and justice disdain them. Let us not speak of them, but do thou look and pass on."

And I, who was gazing, saw a banner, which, whirling, ran so swiftly that it seemed to me disdainful of any pause, and behind it came so long a train of folk, that I should never have believed death had undone so many. After I had recognized some among them, I saw and knew the shade of him who made, through cowardice, the great refusal.[1] At once I understood and was certain, that this was the sect of the caitiffs displeasing to God and to his enemies. These wretches, who never were alive, were naked, and much stung by gad-flies and by wasps that were there; these streaked their faces with blood, which, mingled with tears, was gathered at their feet by loathsome worms.

And when I gave myself to looking onward, I saw people on the bank of a great river; wherefore I said: "Master, now grant to me that I may know who these are, and what rule makes them appear so ready to pass over, as I discern through the faint light." And he to me: "The things will be clear to thee, when we shall stay our steps on the sad shore of Acheron." Then with eyes ashamed and downcast, fearing lest my speech might be troublesome to him, far as to the river I refrained from speaking.

And behold! coming toward us in a boat, an old man, white with ancient hair, crying: "Woe to you, wicked souls! hope not ever to see the Heavens! I come to carry you to the other bank, into the eternal darkness, into heat and into frost. And thou who art there, living soul, depart from these that are dead." But when he saw that I did not depart, he said: "By another way, by other ports thou shalt come to the shore, not here, for passage; a lighter bark must carry thee."

And my Leader to him: "Charon,[2] vex not thyself; it

is thus willed there where is power for that which is willed; and ask no more." Thereon were quiet the fleecy jaws of the ferryman of the livid marsh, who round about his eyes had wheels of flame.

But those souls, who were weary and naked, changed color and gnashed their teeth, soon as they heard his cruel words. They blasphemed God and their parents, the human race, the place, the time and the seed of their sowing and of their birth. Then, all of them bitterly weeping, drew together to the evil bank, which awaits every man who fears not God. Charon the demon, with eyes of glowing coal, beckoning to them, collects them all; he beats with his oar whoever lingers.

As in autumn the leaves depart one after the other, until the bough sees all its spoils upon the earth, in like wise the evil seed of Adam throw themselves from that shore one by one, at signals, as the bird at his recall. Thus they go over the dusky wave, and before they have landed on the farther side, already on this a new throng is assembled.

"My son," said the courteous Master, "those who die in the wrath of God, all come together here from every land; and they are eager to pass over the stream, for the divine justice spurs them so that fear is turned to desire. A good soul never passes this way; and therefore if Charon fret at thee, well mayest thou now know what his speech signifies."

This ended, the gloomy plain trembled so mightily, that the memory of the terror even now bathes me with sweat. The tearful land gave forth a wind that flashed a crimson light which vanquished all sensation in me, and I fell as a man whom slumber seizes.

CANTO IV

The farther side of Acheron.—Virgil leads Dante into Limbo, the First Circle of Hell, containing the spirits of those who lived virtuously but without faith in Christ.—Greeting of Virgil by his fellow poets.—They enter a castle, where are the shades of ancient worthies.—After seeing them Virgil and Dante depart.

A HEAVY THUNDER BROKE the deep sleep in my head, so that I started up like a person who is waked by force, and, risen erect, I moved my rested eye round about, and looked fixedly to distinguish the place where I was. True it is, that I found myself on the brink of the woeful valley of the abyss which collects a thunder of infinite wailings. It was so dark, deep, and cloudy, that, though I fixed my sight on the depth, I did not discern anything there.

16

"Now let us descend here below into the blind world," began the Poet all deadly pale, "I will be first, and thou shalt be second."

And I, who had observed his color, said: "How shall I come, if thou fearest, who art wont to be the comfort to my doubting?" And he to me: "The anguish of the folk who are here below paints on my face that pity which thou takest for fear. Let us go on, for the long way urges us."

Thus he placed himself, and thus he made me enter into the first circle[1] that girds the abyss. Here, as one listened, there was no lamentation but that of sighs which made the eternal air to tremble; this came of the woe without torments felt by the crowds, which were many and great, of infants and of women and of men.

The good Master to me: "Thou dost not ask what spirits are these that thou seest. Now I would have thee know, before thou goest farther, that these did not sin; and though they have merits it suffices not, because they did not have baptism, which is part of the faith that thou believest; and if they were before Christianity, they did not duly worship God: and of such as these am I myself. For such defects, and not for other guilt, are we lost, and only so far harmed that without hope we live in desire."

Great woe seized me at my heart when I heard him, because I knew that people of much worth were suspended in that limbo. "Tell me, my Master, tell me, Lord," I began, with wish to be assured of that faith which vanquishes every error, "did ever any one who afterwards was blessed go forth from here, either by his own or by another's merit?" And he, who understood my covert speech, answered: "I was new in this state when I saw a Mighty One come hither crowned with sign of victory. He drew out hence the shade of the first parent, of Abel his son, and that of Noah, of Moses the law-giver and obedient, Abraham the patriarch, and David the King, Israel with his father and with his offspring, and with Rachel, for whom he did so much, and many others; and He made them blessed: and I would have thee know that before these, human spirits were not saved."[2]

We ceased not going on because he spoke, but all the while were passing through the wood, the wood, I mean, of crowded spirits; nor yet had our way been long from the place of my slumber, when I saw a fire, which overcame a hemisphere of darkness. We were still a little distant from it, yet not so far but that I could in part discern that honorable folk possessed that place. "O thou who honorest both science and art, who are these, who have such honor that it separates them from the manner of the others?" And he to me: "The honorable renown of them which sounds above in thy life wins grace in heaven which thus advances them." At this a voice was heard by me: "Honor the loftiest Poet! his shade returns which had departed." When the voice had stopped and was quiet, I saw four great shades coming to us; they had a semblance neither sad nor glad. The good Master began to say: "Look at him with that sword in hand who comes before the three, even as lord; he is Homer, the sovereign poet; the next who comes is Horace, the satirist; Ovid is the third, and the last is Lucan. Since each shares with me the name which the single voice sounded, they do me honor, and in that do well."

Thus I saw assembled the fair school of that Lord of the loftiest song who soars above the others like an eagle. After they had discoursed somewhat together, they turned to me with sign of salutation; and my Master smiled thereat. And far more of honor yet they did me, for they made me of their band, so that I was the sixth amid so much wisdom. Thus we went on as far as the light, speaking things concerning which silence is becoming, even as was speech there where I was.

We came to the foot of a noble castle,[3] seven times circled by high walls, defended round about by a fair streamlet. This we passed as if hard ground; through seven gates[4] I entered with these sages; we came to a meadow of fresh verdure. People were there with slow and grave eyes, of great authority in their looks; they spoke seldom, and with soft voices. Thereon we withdrew ourselves upon one side, into an open, luminous, and high place, so that they all could be seen. There before me upon the green enamel were shown to me the great spirits, whom for having seen I inwardly exalt myself.

I saw Electra with many companions, among whom I recognized Hector and Aeneas, Caesar in armor, with his gerfalcon eyes; I saw Camilla and Penthesilea, on the other side I saw the King Latinus, who was sitting with Lavinia his daughter. I saw that Brutus who drove out Tarquin; Lucretia, Julia, Marcia, and Cornelia; and alone, apart, I saw the Saladin. When I raised my brows a little more, I saw the Master of those who know,[5] seated amid the philosophic family; all regard him, all do him honor. Here I saw Socrates and Plato, who in front of the others stand nearest to him; Democritus, who ascribes the world to chance; Diogenes, Anaxago-ras, and Thales, Empedocles, Heraclitus, and Zeno; and I saw the good collector of the qualities, Dioscorides, I mean; and I saw Orpheus, Tully, and Linus, and moral Seneca, Euclid the geometer, and Ptolemy, Hippocrates, Avicenna, and Galen, and Aver-rhoës, who made the great comment. I cannot report of all in full, because the long theme so drives me that many times the speech comes short of the fact.

The company of six is reduced to two. By another way the wise guide leads me out from the quiet into the air that trembles, and I come into a region where is nothing that can give light.

Canto V

The Second Circle, that of Carnal Sinners.—
Minos. Shades renowned of old.—Francesca da
Rimini.

THUS I DESCENDED from the first circle down into the second, which girdles less space, and so much more woe that it goads to wailing. There stands Minos[1] horribly, and snarls; he examines the transgressions at the entrance; he judges, and he sends according as he entwines himself. I mean, that when the ill born soul comes there before him, it confesses itself wholly, and that discerner of the sins sees what place of Hell is for it; he girds himself with his tail so many times as the grades he wills that it be sent down. Always many of them stand before him; they go, in turn, each to the judgment; they speak and hear, and then are whirled below.

"O thou that comest to the woeful inn," said Minos to me, when he saw me, leaving the act of so great an office, "beware how thou enterest, and to whom thou trustest thyself; let not the amplitude of the entrance deceive thee." And my Leader to him: "Wherefore dost thou too cry out? Hinder not his fated going; thus is it willed there where is power for that which is willed; and ask no more."

Now the notes of woe begin to make themselves heard by me; now I am come where much wailing smites me. I had come into a place mute of all light, that bellows as the sea does in a tempest, if it be combated by contrary winds. The infernal hurricane which never rests carries along the spirits with its rapine; whirling and smiting it molests them. When they arrive before its rush, here are the shrieks, the complaint, and the lamentation; here they blaspheme the divine power. I understood that to such torment are condemned the carnal sinners who subject the reason to the appetite. And as their wings bear along the starlings in the cold season in a large and full troop, so did that blast the evil spirits; hither, thither, down, up it carries them; no hope ever comforts them, neither of repose, nor of less pain.

And as the cranes go singing their lays, making in air a long line of themselves, so I saw come, uttering wails, shades borne along by the aforesaid strife. Wherefore I said: "Master, who are these folk whom the black air so castigates?" "The first of those of whom thou wishest to have knowledge," said he to me then, "was empress of many tongues. She was so abandoned to the vice of luxury that lust she made licit in her law, to take away the blame into which she had been brought. She is Semiramis, of whom it is read that she succeeded Ninus and had been his wife; she held the land which the Sultan rules. That other is she[2] who, for love, slew herself, and broke faith to the ashes of Sichaeus; next is Cleopatra, the luxurious. See Helen, for whom so long a time of ill revolved; and see the great Achilles, who fought to the end with love. See Paris, Tristan,—" and more than a thousand shades whom love had parted from our life he showed me, and, pointing to them, named to me.

After I had heard my Teacher name the dames of eld and the cavaliers, pity overcame me, and I was well nigh bewildered. I began: "Poet, willingly would I speak with those two that go together, and seem to be so light upon the wind."[3] And he to me: "Thou shalt see when they are nearer to us, and do thou then pray them by that love which leads them, and they will come." Soon as the wind sways them toward us, I lifted my voice: "O wearied souls, come to speak with us, if Another deny it not."

As doves, called by desire, with wings open and steady, come through the air borne by their will to their sweet nest, these issued from the troop where Dido is, coming to us through the malign air, so strong was the compassionate cry.

"O living creature, gracious and benign, that goest through the black air visiting us who stained the world blood-red, if the King of the universe were a friend we would pray Him for thy peace, since thou hast pity on our perverse ill. Of what it pleases thee to hear, and what to speak, we will hear and we will speak to you, while the wind, as now, is hushed for us. The city where I was born sits upon the seashore, where the Po, with his followers, descends to have peace. Love, which quickly lays hold on gentle heart, seized this one for the fair person that was taken from me, and the mode still hurts me. Love, which absolves no loved one from loving, seized me for the pleasing of him so strongly that, as thou seest, it does not even now abandon me. Love brought us to one death. Cain awaits him who quenched our life." These words were borne to us from them.

Soon as I had heard those injured souls I bowed my face, and held it down so long until the Poet said to me: "What art thou thinking?" When I replied, I began: "Alas! how many sweet thoughts, how great desire, led these unto the woeful pass." Then I turned me again to them, and spoke, and began: "Francesca, thy torments make me sad and piteous to weeping. But tell me, at the time of the sweet sighs, by what and how did love concede to thee to know thy dubious desires?" And she to me: "There is no greater woe than the remembering in misery the happy time, and that thy Teacher knows. But if thou hast so great desire to know the first root of our love, I will do like one who weeps and tells.

"We were reading one day, for delight, of Lancelot, how love constrained him. We were alone and without any suspicion. Many times that reading urged our eyes, and took the color from our faces, but only one point was it that overcame us. When we read of the longed-for smile being kissed by such a lover, this one, who never shall be divided from me, kissed my mouth all trembling. Gallehaut was the book, and he who wrote it. That day we read no farther in it."

While the one spirit said this, the other was so weeping that through pity I swooned as if I had been dying, and fell as a dead body falls.

CANTO VI

The Third Circle, that of the Gluttonous.—Cerberus.
—Ciacco.

AT THE RETURN OF my mind, which had closed itself before the pity of these two kinsfolk, that wholly confounded me with sadness, I see around me new torments and new tormented souls wherever I move, and wherever I turn, and wherever I gaze.

I am in the third circle, that of the eternal, accursed, cold, and heavy rain: its rule and quality are never new. Coarse hail, and dark water, and snow pour down through the tenebrous air; the earth which receives them stinks. Cerberus, a cruel and strange beast, with three throats barks dogwise above the people that are here submerged. He has red eyes, a greasy and black beard, and a big belly, and paws armed with nails: he claws the spirits, bites, and rends them. The rain makes them howl like dogs; of one of their sides they make a screen for the other; the wretched profane ones often turn themselves.

When Cerberus, the great worm, observed us, he opened his mouths, and showed his fangs to us; not a limb had he that he held still. And my Leader opened wide his hands, took some earth, and with full fists threw it into his ravenous gullets. As is the dog that baying craves, and becomes quiet when he bites his food, and is intent and struggles only to devour it, such became those filthy faces of the demon Cerberus, who so thunders at the souls that they would fain be deaf.

We were passing over the shades whom the heavy rain subdues, and were setting our feet upon their vain show which seems a body. They all of them were lying on the ground, except one which raised itself to sit, soon as it saw us passing in front. "O thou who art led through this Hell," it said to me, "recognize me, if thou canst; thou wast made before I was unmade." And I to it: "The anguish which thou hast, perchance withdraws thee from my memory, so that it seems not that I ever saw thee. But tell me who thou art, that art set in a place so woeful, and with such a punishment, that if any other be greater, none is so displeasing." And he to me: "Thy city which is so full of envy that already the sack runs over, held me in it, in the bright life. You, citizens, called me Ciacco; for the pernicious fault of gluttony, as thou seest, I am broken by the rain: and I, wretched soul, am not alone, for all these endure like punishment for like fault:" and he spoke not a word more. I answered him: "Ciacco, thy distress so weighs upon me, that it invites me to weeping; but tell me, if thou knowest, to what will come the citizens of the divided city; if any one in it is just; and tell me the cause why such great discord has assailed it."

And he to me: "After long contention they will come to blood, and the sylvan party will chase out the other with much injury. Then afterwards within three suns it behoves that this shall fall, and the other surmount by means of the force of a certain one who just now is tacking. It will hold high its front long time keeping the other under heavy weights, however it may lament and be shamed thereat. There are two just men, but they are not heeded there; Pride, Envy, and Avarice are the three sparks that have inflamed their hearts." Here he made ending of the grievous sound.

And I to him: "I would that thou instruct me further, and that of more speech thou make a gift to me. Farinata and Tegghiaio who were so worthy, Jacopo Rusticucci, Arrigo, and Mosca, and the others who set their minds on well-doing, tell me where they are, and make me to know of them, for great desire urges me to learn if Heaven sweeten them, or Hell envenom them."

And he: "They are among the blacker souls: different sin weighs them down toward the bottom; if thou descend so far, thou mayst see them. But when thou shalt be in the sweet world I pray thee that thou bring me to the memory of others: more I say not to thee, and more I answer thee not." Thereon he twisted his straight eyes awry, looked at me a little, and then bent his head, and fell with it level with the other blind.

And the Leader said to me: "He rouses up no more on this side the sound of the angelic trump. When the hostile Power shall come, each one will find again his dismal tomb, will resume his flesh and his shape, will hear that which through eternity reverberates."

Thus we passed along with slow steps through the foul mixture of the shades and of the rain, touching a little on the future life; wherefore I said: "Master, these torments will they increase after the great Sentence, or be less, or will they be just as burning?" And he to me: "Return to thy science,[1] which declares that in proportion the thing is more perfect the more it feels the good, and so the pain. Though this accursed folk never can attain to true perfection, it expects thereafter to be more than now."

We took a circling course along that road, speaking far more than I repeat; and came to the point where the descent is. Here we found Pluto,[2] the great enemy.

CANTO VII

The Fourth Circle, that of the Avaricious and the Prodigal.—Pluto.—Fortune.
The Styx.—The Fifth Circle, that of the Wrathful.

P*APE SATAN, PAPE SATAN ALEPPE,"* began Pluto with his clucking voice. And that gentle Sage, who knew everything, said to comfort me: "Let not thy fear hurt thee; for, whatever power he have, he shall not take from thee the descent of this rock." Then he turned to that swollen lip and said: "Be silent, accursed wolf![1] consume thyself inwardly with thine own rage: not without cause is this going to the depth; it is willed on high, there where Michael wrought the vengeance for the proud rape." As sails swollen by the wind fall in a heap when the mast snaps, so fell to earth the cruel wild-beast.

Thus we descended into the fourth hollow, taking

more of the woeful bank which insacks the evil of the whole universe. Ah, justice of God! who heaps up so many new travails and penalties as I saw? And why does our guilt so ruin us? As does the wave, yonder upon Charybdis, which is broken on that which it encounters, so needs must here the people counterdance.

Here I saw many more people than elsewhere, both on the one side and the other, with great howls rolling weights by force of chest. They struck against each other, and then there each wheeled round, rolling back, crying: "Why boldest thou?" and "Why flingest thou away?" Thus they turned through the dark circle on either hand to the opposite point, still crying out at each other their opprobrious measure; then each wheeled round, when he had come through his half circle to the other joust.

And I, who had my heart as it were pierced through, said: "My Master, now declare to me what folk this is, and if all these tonsured ones on our left were clerks."

And he to me: "Each and all of these were so asquint in mind in the first life that they made no spending in it with due measure. Clearly enough their voice bays it forth, when they come to the two points of the circle where the contrary fault divides them. These were clerks who have no hairy covering on their heads, and Popes and Cardinals, in whom avarice practices its excess."

And I: "Master, among such as these I ought surely to recognize some who were polluted with these evils."

And he to me: "Thou harborest a vain thought; the undiscerning life that made them foul now makes them dim to all discernment. Forever will they come to the two buttings; these will rise from the sepulchre with closed fist, and these with shorn hair. Ill-giving and ill-keeping have taken from them the beautiful world, and set them to this scuffle; what that is, I adorn not words for it. Now, son, thou canst see the brief jest of the goods that are committed to Fortune, for which the human race struggle with each other; for all the gold that is beneath the moon, or that ever was, could not of these weary souls make a single one repose."

"Master," said I to him, "now tell me further, this Fortune, on which thou touchest to me, what is it, which has the goods of the world so in its clutches?"

And he to me: "O foolish creatures, how great is that ignorance which harms you! I would have thee now receive my opinion concerning her. He whose wisdom transcends all, made the heavens, and gave them their guides, so that every part shines on every part, distributing equally the light. In like wise for the splendors of the world, He ordained a general ministress and guide, who should from time to time transfer the vain goods from race to race, and from one blood to another, beyond the resistance of human wit. Wherefore one race rules, and another languishes, pursuant to her judgment, which is hidden like the snake in the grass. Your wisdom has no withstanding of her: she foresees, judges, and pursues her reign, as theirs the other gods. Her permutations have no truce; necessity compels her to be swift, so often comes he who obtains a turn. This is she who is so set upon the cross, even by those who ought to give her praise, giving her blame amiss and ill report. But she is blessed and hears this not: with the other Primal Creatures glad she turns her sphere, and blessed she rejoices. Now let us descend at once to greater woe: already every star is sinking that was rising when I set out, and too long stay is forbidden."

We crossed the circle to the other bank, above a fount that bubbles up and pours out through a trench which proceeds from it. The water was far darker than perse; and we, in company with the dusky waves, entered down through a strange way. This dismal little stream, when it has descended to the foot of the malign gray slopes, makes a marsh that is named Styx. And I, who was standing intent to gaze, saw muddy people in that swamp, all naked and with look of hurt. They were smiting each other, not with hand only, but with the head, with the chest, and with the feet, mangling one another piecemeal with their teeth.

The good Master said: "Son, now thou seest the souls of those whom anger overcame; and also I will that thou believe for certain that under the water are folk who sigh, and make this water bubble at the surface, as thine eye tells thee wherever it turns. Fixed in the slime, they say: 'Sullen were we in the sweet air that is gladdened by the Sun, bearing within ourselves the sluggish fume; now we are sullen in the black mire.' This hymn they gurgle in their throats, for they cannot speak with entire words.[2]

Thus we circled a great arc of the foul fen, between the dry bank and the slough, with eyes turned on those who guzzle the mire. We came at length to the foot of a tower.

Canto VIII

The Fifth Circle.—Phlegyas and his boat.—Passage of the Styx.—Filippo Argenti.—The City of Dis.—The demons refuse entrance to the poets.

I SAY, CONTINUING, that, long before we were at the foot of the high tower, our eyes went upward to its top by reason of two flamelets that we saw set there, while another was giving signal back from so far off that the eye could hardly catch it. And I turned me to the Sea of all wisdom; I said: "This one, what says it? and what answers that other fire? and who are they that made it?" And he to me: "Upon the turbid waves already thou mayst discern that which is expected, if the fume of the marsh hide it not from thee."

Bowstring never urged arrow from itself that ran so swift a course through the air, as a little vessel which at that instant I saw coming through the water toward us,

34

under the guidance of a single boatman, who cried out: "Now art thou arrived, fell soul?"

"Phlegyas,[1] Phlegyas, this time thou criest out in vain," said my Lord, "thou shalt not have us longer than only while crossing the slough." As one who listens to some great deception that has been practiced on him, and then repines thereat, such became Phlegyas in his gathered anger.

My Leader descended into the bark and then he made me enter after him, and only when I was in did it seem laden. Soon as my Leader and I were in the boat, the antique prow goes its way, cutting more of the water than it is wont with others.

While we were running through the dead channel, one full of mud set himself before me, and said: "Who art thou that comest before thine hour?" And I to him: "If I come, I do not stay; but who art thou that art become so foul?" He answered: "Thou seest that I am one who laments." And I to him, "With lamenting and with sorrow, accursed spirit, do thou remain, for I know thee, though thou be all filthy." Then he stretched to the boat both his hands, whereat the wary Master thrust him back, saying: "Away there, with the other dogs!" Then he clasped my neck with his arms, kissed my face, and said: "Indignant soul, blessed be she who bore thee! That was an arrogant person in the world; no goodness is there that adorns his memory; so is his shade furious here. How many now up there are held great kings who shall lie here like swine in mire, leaving of themselves horrible dispraises!" And I: "Master, I should much like to see him soused in this broth before we depart from the lake." And he to me: "Before the shore lets itself be seen by thee thou shalt be satisfied; it is fitting that thou enjoy such a desire." A little after this I saw such rending of him by the muddy folk that I still praise God therefor, and thank Him for it. All cried: "At Filippo Argenti!" and the raging Florentine spirit turned upon himself with his teeth. Here we left him; so that I tell no more of him.

But on my ears a wailing smote, whereat forward intent I unbar my eye. And the good Master said: "Now, son, the city draws near that is named Dis,[2] with its heavy citizens, with its great throng." And I: "Master, already in the valley therewithin I clearly discern its mosques vermilion, as if they were issuing from fire." And he said to me: "The eternal fire that blazes there within displays them red as thou seest in this nether Hell."

We at last arrived within the deep ditches which encompass that disconsolate city. The walls seemed to me to be of iron. Not without first making a great circuit did we come to a place where the boatman loudly shouted to us: "Get ye out, here is the entrance."

Upon the gates I saw more than a thousand of those rained down from heaven[3] who angrily were saying: "Who is this, that without death goes through the realm of the dead folk?" And my wise Master made a sign of wishing to speak secretly with them. Then they shut in a little their great scorn, and said: "Come thou alone, and let him be gone who so boldly entered on this realm. Alone let him return on the mad path: let him try if he can; for thou, who hast escorted him through so dark a region, shalt remain here."

Think, Reader, if I was discomforted at the sound of

the accursed words, for I did not believe ever to return hither.

"O my dear Leader, who more than seven times hast restored to me security, and drawn me from deep peril that stood confronting me, leave me not," said I, "thus undone; and, if the passing farther onward be denied us, let us together quickly retrace our steps." And that Lord who had led me thither said to me: "Fear not, for no one can take from us our passage, by Such an one is it given to us. But here await me, and comfort thy dejected spirit and feed on good hope, for I will not leave thee in the nether world."

So the sweet Father goes away, and here abandons me, and I remain in suspense; and yes and no contend within my head. I could not hear what he proffered to them, but he had not staid there with them long, when vying with each other they ran back within. These our adversaries closed the gates on the breast of my Lord, who remained without, and turned back to me with slow steps. He had his eyes upon the ground, and his brows were shorn of all hardihood, and he was saying with sighs: "Who has denied to me the houses of woe?" And he said to me: "Because I am wroth, be not thou dismayed, for I shall win the contest, whoever circle round within for the defence. This their insolence is not new, for of old they used it at a less secret gate, which still is found without a bolt. Above it thou didst see the dead inscription; and already, on this side of it, is descending the steep, passing without escort through the circles, One such that by him the city shall be opened to us."

Canto IX

THAT COLOR WHICH cowardice painted outwardly on me when I saw my Guide turn back, repressed more speedily his own new color.[1] He stopped attentive, like a man that listens, for the eye could not lead him far through the black air, and through the dense fog.

"Yet it shall be for us to win the fight," began he, "unless— Such an one offered herself to us. Oh how long it is to me till Another arrive here!"

I saw well how he covered up the beginning with the rest that came after, which were words different from the first; but nevertheless his speech gave me fear, because I drew his broken phrase perchance to a worse meaning than it held.

38

"Into this depth of the dismal shell does any one ever descend from the first grade who has for penalty only hope cut off?" This question I put, and he answered me: "Seldom it happens that any one of us makes the journey on which I am going. It is true that another time I was down here, conjured by that cruel Erichtho[2] who was wont to call back shades into their bodies. Short while had my flesh been bare of me, when she made me enter within that wall, in order to draw thence a spirit of the circle of Judas. That is the lowest place, and the darkest, and the farthest from the Heaven which encircles all. I know the road well; therefore assure thyself. This marsh which breathes out the great stench girds round the woeful city wherein now we cannot enter without anger."

And more he said, but I have it not in mind, because my eye had wholly attracted me toward the high tower with the ruddy summit, where in an instant were uprisen suddenly three infernal Furies,[3] stained with blood, who had the limbs of women and their action, and were girt with greenest hydras. They had for hair little serpents and cerastes, wherewith their savage brows were bound.

And he, who well recognized the handmaids of the queen of the eternal lamentation, said to me: "Behold the fell Erinnyes; this is Megaera on the left side, she who wails on the right is Alecto, Tisiphone is in the middle:" and therewith he was silent.

With her nails each was tearing her breast; they were beating themselves with their hands, and crying out so loud that I pressed close to the Poet through dread.

"Let Medusa come, so we will make him of stone," they all said, looking downward; "ill was it we avenged not on Theseus his assault."

"Turn thee round backwards, and keep thy sight closed, for if the Gorgon[4] show herself, and thou shouldst see her, no return upward would there ever be." Thus said the Master, and he himself turned me, and trusted not to my hands but with his own he also blinded me.

O ye who have sound understandings, regard the doctrine that is hidden under the veil of the strange verses!

And already across the turbid waves was coming a crash of a sound full of terror, at which both the shores trembled. Not otherwise it was than of a wind, impetuous by reason of the opposing heats, which strikes the forest, and without any stay shatters the branches, beats down and carries them away; forward, laden with dust, it goes superb, and makes the wild beasts and the shepherds fly.

My eyes he loosed, and said, "Now direct the nerve of sight across that ancient scum, there yonder where that fume is most bitter."

As the frogs before the hostile snake all vanish through the water, till each huddles on the ground, I saw more than a thousand destroyed souls flying thus before One, who on foot was passing over the Styx with soles unwet. From his face he was removing that thick air, waving his left hand oft before him, and only with that trouble he seemed weary. Well I perceived that he was a messenger from Heaven, and I turned me to the Master, and he made sign that I should stand quiet and bow down to him. Ah, how full of disdain he seemed to me! He came to the gate and with a little rod he opened it, for it had no resistance.

"O outcasts from Heaven! folk despised," began he upon the horrible threshold, "whence is this overweening harbored in you? Wherefore do ye kick against that Will from which its end can never be cut short, and which many a time has increased your woe? What avails it to butt against the fates? Your Cerberus, if ye remember well, still bears his chin and his throat peeled therefor." Then he turned back over the filthy road, and said no word to us, but wore the semblance of a man whom other care constrains and stings, than that of him who is before him.

Then we moved our feet toward the city, secure after his holy words. We entered there within without any strife: and I, who had desire to observe the condition which such a stronghold locks in, soon as I was within, send my eye round about, and I see on every hand a great plain full of woe and of cruel torment.

As at Arles, where the Rhone stagnates, as at Pola, near the Quarnaro which shuts Italy in and bathes her borders, the sepulchres make all the place uneven; so did they here on every side, save that the manner was more bitter here; for among the tombs flames were scattered, by which they were so wholly heated that no art requires iron more so. All their lids were lifted; and such dire laments were issuing forth from them as truly seemed of wretches and of sufferers.

And I: "Master, who are these folk that, buried within those coffers, make themselves heard with their woeful sighs?" And he to me: "Here are the heresiarchs with their followers of every sect, and the tombs are much more laden than thou thinkest. Like with like is buried here, and the monuments are more and less hot."

And after he had turned to the right hand, we passed between the torments and the high battlements.

CANTO X

The Sixth Circle: Heresiarchs—Farinata degli Uberti.—Cavalcante Cavalcanti.—Frederick II.

Now, ALONG A solitary path between the wall of the city and the torments, my Master goes on, and I behind his shoulders.

"O virtue supreme," I began, "that through the impious circles dost turn me according to thy pleasure, speak to me and satisfy my desires. The folk that are lying in the sepulchres, might they be seen? all the lids are now lifted, and no one keeps guard." And he to me: "All will be locked in when they shall return here from Jehoshaphat[1] with the bodies which they have left on earth. Upon this side Epicurus with all his followers, who make the soul mortal with the body, have their burial place. Therefore as to the request that thou makest of me, thou shalt soon be satisfied here within; and

also as to the desire of which thou art silent to me." And
I: "Good Leader, I hold not my heart hidden from thee
except in order to speak little; and not only now hast
thou disposed me to this."

"O Tuscan, who goest thy way alive through the city
of fire, speaking thus modestly, may it please thee to
stop in this place. Thy mode of speech makes manifest
that thou art native of that noble fatherland to which
perchance I was too molestful." Suddenly this sound
issued from one of the coffers, wherefore in fear I
drew a little nearer to my Leader. And he said to me:
"Turn thee: what art thou doing? See there Farinata[2]
who has risen erect; all from the girdle upwards wilt
thou see him."

I had already fixed my face on his, and he was
straightening himself up with breast and front as
though he had Hell in great scorn. And the bold and
ready hands of my Leader pushed me among the sepul-
chres to him, saying: "Let thy words be clear."

When I was at the foot of his tomb, he looked at
me a little, and then, as though disdainful, asked me,
"Who were thy ancestors?" I, who was desirous to
obey, concealed it not from him, but disclosed it all to
him; whereon he raised up his brows a little, then
said: "They were fiercely adverse to me and to my
forefathers and to my party, so that at two times I
scattered them." "If they were driven out, they re-
turned from every side," replied I to him, "both the
one and the other time, but yours have not learned
well that art."

Then there arose to sight alongside of this one, a
shade uncovered far as to the chin: I think that it had

risen on its knees. It looked round about me, as if it had desire to see if another were with me, but when its expectancy was quite spent, weeping it said: "If through this blind prison thou goest by reason of loftiness of genius, where is my son? and why is he not with thee?" And I to him: "I come not of myself; he who waits yonder is leading me through here, whom perchance your Guido had in disdain."

His words and the mode of the punishment had already read to me the name of this one; wherefore my answer was so full.

Suddenly straightening up, he cried: "How didst thou say, 'he had'? lives he not still? does not the sweet light strike his eyes?" When he became aware of some delay that I made before answering, he fell again supine, and appeared no more outside.

But that other magnanimous one, at whose instance I had stayed, changed not aspect, nor moved his neck, nor bent his side. "And if," he said, continuing his first discourse, "they have ill learned that art, it torments me more than this bed. But the face of the Lady[3] who rules here will not be rekindled fifty times ere thou shalt know how much that art weighs. And, so mayest thou return to the sweet world, tell me wherefore is that people so pitiless against my party in its every law?" Thereon I to him: "The rout and the great carnage which colored the Arbia red cause such prayer to be made in our temple." After he had, sighing, shaken his head, "In that I was not alone," he said, "nor surely without cause would I have moved with the others; but I was alone there, where it was agreed by every one to destroy Florence, he who defended her with open face." "Ah! so may your seed ever have repose," I prayed to him, "loose for me that knot, which has here entangled my judgment. It seems, if I hear rightly, that ye see in advance that which time is bringing with it, and as to the present have another way." "We see," he said, "like him who has bad light, the things that are far from us, so much the supreme Ruler still shines on us; when they draw near, or are, our intelligence is wholly vain, and, if another report not to us, we know nothing of your human state; wherefore thou canst comprehend that our knowledge will be utterly dead from that moment when the gate of the future shall be closed." Then, as compunctious for my fault, I said: "Now, then, you will tell to that fallen one that his son is still conjoined with the living, and if just now I was dumb to answer, make him know that I was so because I was already thinking in the error which you have solved for me."

And now my Master was recalling me, wherefore more hastily I prayed the spirit that he would tell me who was with him. He said to me: "Here I lie with more than a thousand; here within is the second Frederick and the Cardinal, and of the others I am silent."

Thereon he hid himself; and I turned my steps toward the ancient Poet, reflecting on that speech which seemed hostile to me. He moved on, and then, thus going, he said to me: "Why art thou so disturbed?" And I satisfied him as to his question. "Let thy memory preserve that which thou hast heard against thyself," that Sage bade me, "and now give heed here—" and he raised his finger: "When thou shalt be in presence of the sweet radiance of her whose beautiful eye sees everything, from her thou shalt learn the journey of thy life." Then to the left he turned his step.

We left the wall, and went toward the middle by a path that strikes into a valley which even up there was making its stench displeasing.

Canto XI

The Sixth Circle: Heretics.—Tomb of Pope Anastasius.—Discourse of Virgil on the divisions of the lower Hell.

UPON THE EDGE of a high bank which great rocks broken in a circle made, we came above a more cruel pen. And here, because of the horrible excess of the stench which the deep abyss throws out, we drew aside behind the lid of a great tomb, whereon I saw an inscription which said: "I hold Pope Anastasius, whom Photinus drew from the right way."

"It behoves that our descent be slow, so that the sense may first accustom itself a little to the dismal blast, and then it will be of no concern." Thus the Master, and I said to him: "Some compensation do thou find that the time pass not lost." And he: "Behold, I am thinking of that. My son, within these rocks," he began then to say, "are three lesser circles from grade to grade, like those which thou art leaving. All are full of accursed spirits; but, in order that hereafter the sight alone may suffice thee, hear how and wherefore they are in bonds.

"Of every wickedness[1] that acquires hate in heaven injury is the end, and every such end afflicts others either by force or by fraud. But because fraud is an evil peculiar to man, it more displeases God; and therefore the fraudulent are the lower, and woe assails them more.

"The first circle is wholly of the violent: but because violence is done to three persons, it is divided and constructed in three rounds. To God, to one's self, to one's neighbor may violence be done; I say to them and to their belongings, as thou shalt hear with plain discourse. By violence, death and grievous wounds are inflicted on one's neighbor; and on his substance ruins, burnings, and harmful extortions. Wherefore the first round torments homicides, and every one who smites wrongfully, all despoilers and plunderers, in various troops.

"Man may lay violent hands upon himself and on his goods; and, therefore, in the second round it behoves that he repent without avail who deprives himself of your world, gambles away and dissipates his property, and laments there where he ought to be joyous.

"Violence may be done to the Deity, by denying and blaspheming Him in the heart, and by contemning nature and His bounty: and therefore the smallest round seals with its signet both Sodom and Cahors,[2] and him who, contemning God, speaks from his heart.

"The fraud, by which every conscience is stung, man may practice on one that confides in him, or on one that has no stock of confidence. This latter mode seems to destroy only the bond of love which nature makes;[3] wherefore in the second circle nest hypocrisy, flatteries, and he who bewitches, falsity, robbery, and simony, panders, barrators, and such like filth.

"By the other mode that love is forgotten which nature makes and that which is thereafter added, whereby special confidence is created. Hence, in the smallest circle, where is the point of the universe, upon which Dis sits, whoso betrays is consumed forever."

And I: "Master, full clearly thy discourse proceeds, and full well divides this pit, and the people that possess it; but, tell me, they of the fat marsh, and they whom the wind drives, and they whom the rain beats, and they who encounter with such rough tongues, why are they not punished within the ruddy city[4] if God be wroth with them? and if he be not so, why are they in such plight?"

And he said to me: "Why does thy wit so wander beyond its wont? or thy mind, where else is it gazing? Dost thou not remember those words with which thy Ethics treats in full of the three dispositions that Heaven abides not; incontinence, wickedness, and mad bestiality, and how incontinence less offends God, and incurs less blame? If thou consider well this doctrine, and bring to mind who are those that up above suffer punishment outside, thou wilt see clearly why they are divided from these felons, and why less wroth the divine vengeance hammers them."

"O Sun that healest every troubled vision, thou dost

content me so, when thou solvest, that doubt, not less than knowledge, pleases me; yet turn thee a little back," said I, "to where thou sayest that usury offends the Divine Goodness,[5] and loose the knot."

"Philosophy," he said to me, "points out to him who understands it, not only in one part alone, how Nature takes her course from the Divine Intellect and from Its art. And if thou note thy Physics[6] well thou wilt find, after not many pages, that your art follows her so far as it can, as the disciple does the master, so that your art is as it were grandchild of God. From these two, if thou bring to mind Genesis at its beginning,[7] it behoves mankind to gain their life and to advance. But because the usurer holds another way, he contemns Nature in herself, and in her follower, since upon other thing he sets his hope.[8] But follow me now, for to go on pleases me; for the Fishes are quivering on the horizon, and the Wain lies quite over Caurus, and far onwards is the descent of the steep."

CANTO XII

—✦—

The Seventh Circle, first round: those who do vio-
lence to others.—The Minotaur.—The Cen-
taurs.—Chiron.—Nessus.—The River of boiling
Blood, and the Sinners in it.

THE PLACE WHERE we came to descend the bank
was alpine, and, because also of what was there,
such that every eye would be shy of it.

As is that downfall which, on this side of Trent,
struck the Adige on its flank, either by earthquake or
through failure of support,—for from the top of the
mountain, whence it started, to the plain, the cliff has
so tumbled down that it might afford some path to one
that were above—such was the descent of that ravine:
and on the edge of the broken chasm was outstretched
the infamy of Crete,[1] that was conceived in the false
cow. And when he saw us he bit himself even as one

whom wrath rends inwardly. My Sage cried out toward him: "Perchance thou believest that here is the Duke of Athens,[2] who up in the world gave thee thy death? Get thee gone, beast, for this one does not come instructed by thy sister, but he goes to behold your punishments."

As is that bull which breaks his halter at the instant he has just received his mortal stroke, and cannot go, but plunges this way and that, I saw the Minotaur do the like.

And he watchful cried: "Run to the pass; while he is in a rage it is well that thou descend." So we took our way down over the discharge of those stones, which often moved under my feet because of the novel burden.

I was going along thinking, and he said: "Thou art thinking perhaps on this ruin which is guarded by that bestial wrath which I just now quelled. Now I would have thee know that the other time when I descended here below into the nether hell, this cliff had not yet fallen. But in truth, if I discern aright, a little ere He came, who levied the great spoil on Dis from the uppermost circle, on all sides the deep foul valley trembled so that I thought the universe felt love whereby, as some believe, the world has oft-times been converted into chaos: and, at that moment, this ancient rock here and elsewhere made such downfall. But fix thine eyes below, for the river of blood is near, in which everyone who does harm by violence to others is boiling."

Oh blind cupidity, both guilty and mad, which so spurs us in the short life, and then, in the eternal, steeps us so ill!

I saw a broad ditch, according as my Guide had said,

bent in an arc, as that which embraces all the plain.
And between the foot of the bank and it, Centaurs were
running in a file, armed with arrows, as they were wont
in the world to go to the chase. Seeing us descending,
each stopped, and from the troop three detached them-
selves, with bows and darts first selected. And one cried
from afar: "To what torment are ye coming, ye who de-
scend the slope? Tell it from there; if not, I draw the
bow." My Master said: "We will make answer unto Chi-
ron near by there: to thy hurt was thy will ever thus
hasty."

Then he touched me, and said: "That is Nessus, who
died for the beautiful Dejanira, and himself wrought
vengeance for himself; and that one in the middle, who
is gazing on his own breast, is the great Chiron who
nurtured Achilles; that other is Pholus, who was so full
of wrath. Round about the ditch they go by thousands,
shooting with their arrows whatever soul lifts itself from
the blood more than its crime has allotted to it."

We drew near to those fleet wild beasts. Chiron took
a shaft, and with the notch put his beard back upon his
jaws. When he had thus uncovered his great mouth he
said to his companions: "Are ye aware that the one be-
hind moves what he touches? thus are not wont to do
the feet of the dead." And my good Leader, who was
now at his breast, where the two natures are conjoined,
replied: "He is indeed alive, and thus alone it behoves
me to show him the dark valley: necessity leads him and
not delight. One who withdrew from singing hallelujah
committed unto me this new duty; he is no robber, nor
I a fraudulent soul. But, by that Power through which I
move my steps along so savage a road, give to us one of

thine, to whom we may keep close, who may show us
where the ford is, and may carry this one on his back,
who is not a spirit that can go through the air."

Chiron turned upon his right breast, and said to Nes-
sus: "Turn, and guide them thus, and if another troop
encounter you, make it give way."

We moved on with the trusty escort along the edge
of the crimson boiling, in which the boiled were utter-
ing loud shrieks. I saw folk under it up to the brow, and
the great Centaur said: "These are tyrants who laid hold
on blood and plunder. Here they bewail their merciless
misdeeds: here is Alexander, and cruel Dionysius who
made Sicily have woeful years. And that forehead which
has such black hair is Azzolino, and that other who is
blond is Opizzo of Este, who of a truth was slain by his
stepson up there in the world."

Then I turned me to the Poet, and he said: "Let him
now be first for thee, and I second." A little further on
the Centaur stopped above a folk who far as the throat
seemed to come out from that boiling stream. He
showed to us at one side a solitary shade, and said: "He
cleft, in the bosom of God, the heart that still is hon-
ored on the Thames."[3] Then I saw folk, who were hold-
ing their heads, and even all their chests, out of the
stream; and of these I recognized many. Thus more and
more that blood sank down, until it cooked only the
feet: and here was our passage of the foss.

"As on this hand, thou seest that the boiling stream
continually diminishes," said the Centaur, "so I would
have thee believe that on this other it lowers its bed
more and more, until it comes round again to where it
behoves that tyranny should groan. The divine justice

here goads that Attila who was a scourge on earth, and Pyrrhus and Sextus; and forever milks the tears which with the boiling it unlocks from Rinier of Corneto and from Rinier Pazzo,[4] who made such warfare upon the highways."

Then he turned back and repassed the ford.

Canto XIII

---❦---

The Seventh Circle, second round: those who have done violence to themselves and to their goods.— The Wood of Self-murderers.—The Harpies.— Pier delle Vigne.—Lano of Siena and others.

Nessus had not yet reached the yonder bank when we set forward through a wood which was marked by no path. Not green leaves were there, but of a dusky color, not smooth boughs but gnarled and tangled, not fruits but thorns with poison. Those savage wild-beasts that hold in hate the tilled places between Cecina and Corneto have no thickets so rough or so dense.

Here the foul Harpies make their nests, who chased the Trojans from the Strophades with dismal announcement of future calamity. They have broad wings, and human necks and faces, feet with claws, and the great belly feathered. They make lament on the strange trees.

And the good Master began to say to me: "Before thou enterest farther, know that thou art in the Second Round, and wilt be, till thou shalt come to the horrible sand. Therefore look well around, and so shalt thou see things that would take credence from my speech."[1]

I heard wailings uttered on every side, and I saw no one who made them, wherefore, all bewildered, I stopped. I believe that he believed that I believed that all these voices issued from amid those trunks from people who because of us had hidden themselves. Therefore said the Master: "If thou break off any twig from one of these plants, the thoughts thou hast will all be cut short." Then I stretched my hand a little forward and plucked a little branch from a great thorn-bush, and its trunk cried out: "Why dost thou break me?" When it had become dark with blood it began again to cry: "Why dost thou tear me? hast thou not any spirit of pity? Men we were, and now we are become stocks; truly thy hand ought to be more pitiful had we been souls of serpents."

As from a green log that is burning at one of its ends, and drips from the other, and hisses with the air that is escaping, so from that broken twig came out words and blood together; whereon I let the tip fall, and stood like a man who is afraid.

"If he had been able to believe before," replied my Sage, "O injured soul, what he has seen only in my verse, he would not have stretched out his hand on thee; but the incredible thing made me prompt him to an act which weighs on me myself. But tell him who thou wast, so that, by way of some amends, he may refresh thy fame in the world above, whereto it is allowed him to return."

And the trunk:[2] "Thou dost so allure me with sweet speech, that I cannot be silent, and may it not burden you, that I am enticed to talk a little. I am he who held both the keys of the heart of Frederick, and who turned them, locking and unlocking so softly, that from his secrets I kept almost every one. Fidelity so great I bore to the glorious office, that I lost my sleep and my pulse thereby. The harlot,[3] that never from the abode of Cæsar turned her strumpet eyes,—the common death and vice of courts,—inflamed all minds against me, and they, inflamed, did so inflame Augustus that my glad honors turned to dismal sorrows. My mind, through scornful disgust, thinking to escape scorn by death, made me unjust toward my just self. By the strange roots of this tree I swear to you, that I never broke faith to my lord who was so worthy of honor. And if one of you returns to the world, let him comfort my memory which yet lies prostrate from the blow that envy gave it."

He paused a little, and then, "Since he is silent," said the Poet to me, "lose not the hour, but, if more please thee, speak and enquire of him." Whereon I to him: "Do thou ask him further of what thou thinkest may satisfy me, for I cannot, such great pity fills my heart."

Therefore he began again: "So may this man do for thee freely that which thy speech prays for, spirit incarcerate, may it please thee yet to tell us how the soul is bound within these knots, and tell us, if thou canst, if from such limbs any soul is ever loosed."

Then the trunk puffed strongly, and soon the wind

was changed into this voice: "Briefly shall ye be answered. When the ferocious soul departs from the body wherefrom itself has torn itself, Minos sends it to the seventh gulf. It falls into the wood, and no part is chosen for it, but where fortune flings it there it sprouts like a grain of spelt; it rises in a sapling and to a wild plant: the Harpies, feeding then upon its leaves, give pain, and to the pain a window. Like the others we shall go for our spoils, but not, however, that any one may revest himself with them, for it is not just for one to have that of which he deprives himself. Hither shall we drag them, and through the melancholy wood shall our bodies be suspended, each on the thorn-tree of its molested shade."

We were still attentive to the trunk, believing that it might wish to say more to us, when we were surprised by an uproar, like one who perceives the wild boar and the chase coming toward his post, and hears the beasts and the crash of the branches. And behold, two on the left hand, naked and scratched, flying so hard that they broke through every barrier of the wood. The one in front was shouting: "Haste now! haste thee, Death!" and the other, who seemed to himself too slow: "Lano, thy legs were not so nimble at the jousts of the Toppo":[4] and since perhaps his breath was failing, of himself and of a bush he made a group. Behind them the wood was full of black bitches, ravenous and running like greyhounds that had been slipped from the leash. On him who had squatted they set their teeth and tore him piecemeal, then carried off those woeful limbs.

My Guide then took me by the hand, and led me to the bush, which was weeping in vain through its bleeding fractures. "O Jacomo of Sant' Andrea," it was saying, "what has it vantaged thee to make of me a screen? What blame have I for thy wicked life?" When the Master had stopped above it, he said: "Who wast thou, who through so many wounds blowest forth with blood a woeful speech?" And he to us: "O souls that are arrived to see the shameful ravage that has thus disjoined my twigs from me, collect them at the foot of the wretched bush. I was of the city which for the Baptist changed her first patron; wherefore he will always make her sorrowful with his art. And were it not that at the passage of the Arno some semblance of him still remains, those citizens who afterwards rebuilt it upon the ashes that were left by Attila⁵ would have done the work in vain. I made a gibbet for myself of my own house."

CANTO XIV

The Seventh Circle, third round: those who have done violence to God.—The Burning Sand.—Capaneus.—Figure of the Old Man in Crete.—The Rivers of Hell.

BECAUSE THE LOVE of my native place constrained me, I gathered up the scattered twigs and gave them back to him who was already faint-voiced.

Thence we came to the confine, where the second round is divided from the third, and where a horrible mode of justice is seen.

To make the new things clearly manifest, I say that we had reached a plain which rejects every plant from its bed. The woeful wood is a garland round about it, even as the dismal foss to that. Here, on the very edge, we stayed our steps. The floor was an arid and dense sand, not made in other fashion than that which of old was trodden by the feet of Cato.[1]

O vengeance of God, how much shouldst thou be feared by every one who reads that which was manifest to my eyes!

I saw many flocks of naked souls, that were all weeping very miserably, and divers law seemed imposed upon them. Some folk were lying supine on the ground; some were seated all crouched up, and others were going about continually.[2] Those who were going around were the more numerous, and those the less so who were lying down under the torment, but they had their tongues more loosed by the pain.

Over all the sand, with a slow falling, were raining down dilated flakes of fire, as of snow on alps without a wind. As the flames which Alexander in those hot parts of India saw falling upon his host, unbroken to the ground, wherefore he took care to trample the soil by his troops, because the vapor was better extinguished while it was single; so was descending the eternal heat whereby the sand was kindled, like tinder beneath the steel, for doubling of the dole. The dance of the wretched hands was ever without repose, now there, now here, shaking off from them the fresh burning.

I began: "Master, thou that overcomest everything, except the obdurate demons, who at the entrance of the gate came out against us, who is that great one that seems not to heed the fire, and lies despiteful and twisted, so that the rain seems not to ripen him?" And that same one who was aware that I was asking my Leader about him, cried out: "Such as I was alive, such am I dead. Though Jove weary out his smith, from whom in wrath he took the sharp thunderbolt wherewith on my last day I was smitten, or though he weary out the others, turn by turn, in Mongibello at the black forge, crying, 'Good Vulcan, help, help!' even as he did at the fight of Phlegra, and hurl on me with all his might, he should not have thereby glad vengeance."

Then my Leader spoke with force so great, that I had never heard him so vehement: "O Capaneus, in that thy pride is not extinct, art thou the more punished; no torment save thine own rage would be a pain adequate to thy fury."

Then he turned round to me with better look, saying: "That was one of the Seven Kings who besieged Thebes, and he held, and it seems that he holds God in disdain, and it seems that he little prizes Him; but as I said to him, his own despites are very due adornments for his breast. Now come behind me, and take heed still not to set thy feet upon the scorched sand, but keep them always close to the wood."

In silence we came to where a little brook, the redness of which still makes me shudder, gushes forth from the wood. As from the Bulicame³ a rivulet issues, which then the sinful women share among them, so that went down across the sand. Its bed and both its sloping banks were made of stone, and the margins on the side, wherefore I perceived that the crossing was there.

"Among all else that I have shown to thee, since we entered through the gate whose threshold is denied to no one, nothing has been discerned by thine eyes so notable as is the present stream which deadens all the flamelets above it." These words were of my Leader, wherefore I prayed him, that he would bestow on me the food of which he had bestowed on me the desire.

"In mid sea lies a wasted land," said he then, "which is named Crete, under whose king the world of old was chaste. A mountain is there which of old was glad with water and with leaves, which is called Ida; now it is desert, like a thing outworn. Rhea chose it of old for the trusty cradle of her little son, and, the better to conceal him when he wailed, caused cries to be made there. Within the mountain a great old man stands upright, who holds his shoulders turned towards Damietta,[4] and gazes at Rome as if his mirror. His head is formed of fine gold, and his arms and breast are pure silver; then far as to the fork he is of brass; from there downward he is all of chosen iron, save that his right foot is of baked earth, and he stands erect on that more than on the other.[5] Every part except the gold is cleft with a fissure that drips tears, which, collected, perforate that cavern. Their course is from rock to rock into this valley; they form Acheron, Styx, and Phlegethon; then their way is down through this narrow channel till, where there is no more descending, they form Cocytus, and what that pool is, thou shalt see; therefore here it is not told."

And I to him: "If the present stream flows down thus from our world, why does it appear to us only at this border?"

And he to me: "Thou knowest that the place is circular, and though thou art come far, always to the left in descending toward the bottom, thou hast not yet turned through the whole circle; wherefore if a new thing appears to us, it ought not to bring wonder to thy face."

And I again: "Master, where are Phlegethon and Lethe found, for of the one thou art silent, and the other thou sayest is formed by this rain?"

"In all thy questions truly thou pleasest me," he answered, "but the boiling of the red water should well solve one that thou askest. Lethe thou shalt see, but outside of this ditch, there where the souls go to lave themselves, when the fault repented of has been removed." Then he said, "Now it is time to quit the wood; take heed that thou come behind me; the margins which are not burning afford way, and above them every vapor is extinguished."

CANTO XV

Third round of the Seventh Circle: of those who have done violence to Nature.—Brunetto Latini.—Prophecies of misfortune to Dante.

Now ONE OF the hard margins bears us on, and the fume of the brook overshadows so that it saves the water and the banks from the fire. As the Flemings, between Wissant and Bruges, fearing the flood that rushes toward them, make the bulwark whereby the sea may be routed; and as the Paduans along the Brenta, in order to defend their towns and their castles, ere Chiarentana feel the heat,—in such like were these made, though neither so high nor so thick had the master, whoever he was, made them.

We were now so remote from the wood that I could not have seen where it was though I had turned backward, when we encountered a troop of souls which was coming alongside the bank, and each of them was look-ing at us, as a man is wont to look at another at evening under the new moon; and they so sharpened their brows toward us as the old tailor does on the needle's eye.

Thus eyed by that company, I was recognized by one who took me by the hem, and cried out: "What a mar-vel!" And when he stretched out his arm to me, I fixed my eyes on his baked aspect so that his scorched visage did not prevent the recognition of him by my intelli-gence; and bending down my own to his face, I an-swered: "Are you here, Ser Brunetto?" And he: "O my son, let it not displease thee if Brunetto Latini turns back a little with thee, and lets the train go on." I said to him: "With all my power I pray this of you, and if you will that I sit down with you I will do so, if it please him there,[1] for I go with him." "O son," said he, "whoever of this herd stops for an instant, lies afterwards a hundred years without fanning himself when the fire smites him; therefore go onward: I will come at thy skirts, and then I will rejoin my band which goes lamenting its eternal penalties."

I dared not descend from the road to go level with him, but I held my head bowed like one who goes rev-erently. He began: "What fortune or destiny leads thee down here before thy last day? and who is this that shows the road?"

"There above, in the bright life," I answered him, "I went astray in a valley, before my time was full. Only yesterday morning I turned my back on it: this one ap-peared to me as I was returning to it, and he is leading me homeward again along this path."

And he to me: "If thou follow thy star, thou canst not miss the glorious port, if, in the fair life, I discerned aright: and if I had not so untimely died, seeing heaven so benignant to thee, I would have given thee cheer in thy work. But that ungrateful malignant people which descended from Fiesole of old, and still smacks of the mountain and the rock, will make itself hostile to thee because of thy good deeds; and it is right, for among the bitter sorb-trees it befits not the sweet fig to bear fruit. Old report in the world calls them blind; it is an avaricious, envious, and proud folk; from their customs take heed that thou cleanse thyself. Thy fortune reserves such honor for thee that the one party and the other shall have hunger for thee: but far from the goat shall be the grass. Let the Fiesolan beasts make litter of themselves, and let them not touch the plant, if any spring yet upon their dungheap, in which the holy seed may revive of those Romans who remained there when it became the nest of so much wickedness."

"If my entreaty were all fulfilled," replied I to him, "you would not yet be placed in banishment from human nature; for in my mind is fixed, and now fills my heart, the dear, good, paternal image of you, when in the world hour by hour you taught me how man makes himself eternal; and how much I hold it in gratitude, it behoves that while I live should be discerned in my speech. That which you tell of my course I write, and reserve it with other text to be glossed by a Lady, who will know how, if I attain to her. Thus much would I have manifest to you, that I, provided my conscience chide me not, for Fortune, as she wills, am ready. Such earnest[2] is not strange unto my ears; therefore let Fortune turn her wheel as pleases her, and the churl his mattock."

My Master thereupon turned backward to his right, and looked at me; then said: "He listens well who notes it."

Not the less for this do I go on speaking with Ser Brunetto, and I ask, who are his most noted and most eminent companions. And he to me: "To know of some is good, of the others it will be laudable for us to be silent, for the time would be short for so much speech. In brief, know that all were clerks, and great men of letters and of great fame, defiled in the world by one same sin. Priscian goes along with that disconsolate crowd, and Francesco d' Accorso; and thou couldst also have seen there, hadst thou had hankering for such scurf, him who was translated by the Servant of Servants from the Arno to the Bacchiglione, where he left his illstrained nerves. Of more would I tell, but my going on and my speech cannot be longer, for I see yonder a new smoke rising from the sand. Folk come with whom I must not be. Let my Treasure, in which I still am living, be commended to thee, and more I ask not."

Then he turned back, and seemed of those who run across the plain at Verona for the green cloth,[3] and of these he seemed the one that wins, and not he that loses.

CANTO XVI

The Seventh Circle, third round: those who have done violence to Nature.—Guido Guerra, Tegghiaio Aldobrandi and Jacopo Rusticucci.—The roar of Phlegethon as it pours downward.—The cord thrown into the abyss.

I WAS NOW IN a place where the resounding of the water which was falling into the next circle was heard, like that hum which the beehives make, when three shades together separated themselves, as they ran, from a troop that was passing under the rain of the bitter torment. They came toward us, and each cried out: "Stop thou, who by thy garb seemest to us to be one from our wicked city!"

Ah me! what wounds I saw upon their limbs, recent and old, burnt in by the flames; it grieves me still for them but to remember it.

My Teacher gave heed to their cries; he turned his face toward me, and: "Now wait," he said; "to these one should be courteous, and were it not for the fire which the nature of the place shoots forth, I should say that haste better befitted thee than them."

As we stopped, they began again the old verse and when they had reached us they all three made a wheel of themselves. As champions, naked and oiled, are wont to do, watching for their grip and their vantage, before they exchange blows and thrusts, thus, wheeling, each directed his face on me, so that his neck was making continuous journey in contrary direction to his feet.

"And if the wretchedness of this soft place[1] bring us and our prayers into contempt," began one, "and our darkened and scorched aspect, let our fame incline thy mind to tell us who thou art, that so securely rubbest thy living feet through Hell. He whose tracks thou seest me trample, although he go naked and stripped of skin, was of greater degree than thou thinkest. He was grandson of the good Gualdrada; his name was Guido Guerra, and in his life he did much with wisdom and with the sword. The other who treads the sand behind me is Tegghiaio Aldobrandi, whose reputation should be cherished in the world above. And I, who am set with them on the cross, was Jacopo Rusticucci, and surely my savage wife more than aught else injures me."

If I had been sheltered from the fire I should have cast myself below among them, and I believe that the Teacher would have permitted it; but because I should have been burnt and baked, fear overcame my good will which made me greedy to embrace them. Then I began: "Not contempt, but grief, did your condition fix within me, such that slowly will it be all divested, soon as this my Lord said to me words by which I bethought me that such folk as ye are were coming. I am of your city; and I have always rehearsed and heard with affection your deeds and honored names. I am leaving the gall, and going for sweet fruits promised to me by my veracious Leader; but far as to the centre I needs must first descend."

"So may thy soul long direct thy limbs," replied he then, "and so may thy fame shine after thee, say if courtesy and valor abide in our city as of wont, or if they have quite gone forth from it? For Guglielmo Borsiere, who is in torment with us but short while, and is going yonder with our companions, afflicts us greatly with his words."

"The new people and the sudden gains[2] have engendered pride and excess, Florence, in thee, so that already thou weepest therefor." Thus I cried with uplifted face, and the three, who understood this for answer, looked one at the other, as one looks at truth.

"If other times it costs thee so little," replied they all, "to satisfy others, happy thou if thus thou speakest at thy pleasure. Wherefore, if thou escapest from these dark places, and returnest to see again the beautiful stars, when it shall rejoice thee to say, 'I have been,' mind thou tell of us to the people." Then they broke the wheel, and in flying their swift legs seemed wings.

An amen could not have been said so quickly as they had disappeared: wherefore it seemed well to my Master to depart. I followed him, and we had gone little way before the sound of the water was so near to us, that had we spoken we had scarce been heard. As that river which first from Monte Viso holds its own course toward the east, on the left flank of the Apennine,—which is called Acquacheta up above, before it sinks down into its low bed, and at Forlì has lost that name,—reverberates in falling from the alp with a single leap there above San Benedetto, where ought to be shelter for a thousand; thus, down from a precipitous bank, we found that dark water resounding, so that in short while it would have hurt the ears.

I had a cord girt around me, and with it I had once thought to take the leopard of the painted skin.[3] After I had loosed it wholly from me, as my Leader had commanded me, I reached it to him gathered up and coiled. Whereon he turned toward the right, and threw it, somewhat far from the edge, down into that deep gulf. "And surely," said I to myself, "it must be that some novelty respond to the novel signal which the Master so follows with his eye."

Ah! how cautious ought men to be near those who see not only the deed, but with their wisdom look within the thoughts! He said to me: "That which I await will soon come up, and what thy thought is dreaming must soon discover itself to thy sight."

A man ought always to close his lips so far as he can to that truth which has the aspect of falsehood, because without fault it causes shame; but here I cannot be silent, and Reader, I swear to thee, by the notes of this comedy,—so may they not be void of lasting grace,—

that I saw through that thick and dark air a shape marvelous to every steadfast heart come swimming upwards, like as he returns who goes down sometimes to loose an anchor that grapples either a rock or aught else which is hidden in the sea, who stretches upward, and draws in his feet.

CANTO XVII

Third round of the Seventh Circle: of those who have done violence to Art.—Geryon.—The Usurers.—Descent to the Eighth Circle.

"BEHOLD THE WILD BEAST with the pointed tail, that passes mountains, and breaks walls and weapons; behold him that infects all the world."[1] Thus began my Leader to speak to me; and he beckoned to him that he should come to shore near the end of the marbles we had walked on. And that loathsome image of fraud came onward, and landed his head and his bust, but did not draw up his tail on the bank. His face was the face of a just man (so benignant the skin it had outwardly), and all his trunk was of a serpent; he had two paws, hairy to the armpits; his back and his breast and both his sides were painted with nooses and rings. Tartars or Turks never made cloth with more colors of groundwork and pattern, nor were such webs laid on the loom by Arachne.

As sometimes boats lie on the shore, and are partly in water and partly on the ground, and as yonder, among the gluttonous Germans, the beaver settles himself to make his war, so lay that worst of beasts upon the edge of stone which closes in the sand. In the void all his tail was quivering, twisting upwards its venomous fork, which in guise of a scorpion armed the point.

The Leader said: "Now needs must our way bend a little toward that wicked beast which is couching yonder." Therefore we descended on the right hand side and took ten steps upon the verge in order completely to avoid the sand and the flamelets. And when we had come to him, I see, a little farther on, people sitting upon the sand near to the empty space.

Here the Master said to me: "In order that thou mayst carry away quite full experience of this round, now go and see their condition. Let thy talk there be brief; until thou returnest I will speak with this beast, that it may concede to us its strong shoulders."

Thus, further up along the extreme head of that seventh circle, all alone I went where the sad people were sitting. Their woe was bursting forth through their eyes; now here, now there they made help with their hands, sometimes against the vapors, and sometimes against the hot soil. Not otherwise do the dogs in summer, now with muzzle, now with paws, when they are bitten either by fleas, or flies, or gadflies. When I set my eyes on the face of certain of those on whom the grievous fire falls, I did not recognize one of them; but I perceived that from the neck of each was hanging a pouch, which had a certain color and a certain device,[2] and therewith it seems their eye is fed. And as I come gazing among them, I saw upon a yellow purse azure which had the face and bearing of a lion. Then as the current of my look proceeded, I saw another, red as blood, display a goose whiter than butter. And one, who had his little white sack marked with an azure and gravid sow, said to me: "What art thou doing in this ditch? Now get thee gone: and since thou art still alive, know that my neighbor, Vitaliano, will sit here at my left side. With these Florentines am I, a Paduan; often they stun my ears, shouting: 'Let the sovereign cavalier come who will bring the pouch with the three beaks.' " Then he twisted his mouth, and thrust out his tongue, like an ox that licks its nose. And I, fearing lest longer stay might vex him who had admonished me to stay but little, turned back from these weary souls.

I found my Leader, who had already mounted upon the croup of the fierce animal, and he said to me: "Now be thou strong and courageous; henceforth the descent is by such stairs;[3] mount thou in front, for I wish to be between, so that the tail cannot do harm."

As is he who has the shivering fit of the quartan so near that his nails are already pale, and he is all of a tremble only looking at the shade, such I became at these uttered words: but his exhortations wrought shame in me, which in presence of a good lord makes a servant strong.

I seated myself on those huge shoulders. "So do," I

wished to say, but the voice came not as I thought, "that thou embrace me." But he who other time had suc-cored me, in other chance, soon as I mounted, clasped me and sustained me with his arms; and he said: "Geryon, move on now; let thy circles be wide, and thy descending slow; consider the novel burden that thou hast."

As the little vessel goes from its place, backward, backward, so he thence withdrew; and when he felt himself quite at play, he turned his tail to where his breast had been, and moved it stretched out like an eel, and with his paws gathered the air to himself. Greater fear I do not think there was when Phaëthon aban-doned the reins, whereby heaven, as is still apparent, was scorched; nor when the wretched Icarus felt his loins unfeathering by the melted wax, his father crying to him: "Ill way thou holdest," than mine was, when I saw that I was in the air on every side, and saw every sight vanished, except that of the beast. It goes along swimming slowly, slowly, wheels and descends, but I perceive it not, save for the wind upon my face, and from below.

I heard now on the right hand the gulf making be-neath us a horrible din; wherefore I stretch out my head, with my eyes downward. Then I became more terrified at the precipice, because I saw fires and heard laments; whereat I, trembling, all the closer cling. And I saw then, for I had not seen them before, the de-scending and the circling, by the great evils which were drawing near on divers sides.

As the falcon which has been long on wing, that, without sight of lure or bird, makes the falconer say:

"Ah me, thou stoopest!" descends weary, whence it started swiftly, through a hundred circles, and alights disdainful and sullen far from its master; so Geryon set us at the bottom, at the very foot of the rough hewn rock, and, disburdened of our persons, vanished as arrow from the bowstring.

CANTO XVIII

Eighth Circle: the fraudulent; the first pouch: panders and seducers.—Venedico Caccianimico.—Jason.—Second valley: false flatterers.—Alessio Interminei.—Thais.

THERE IS A PLACE in Hell called Malebolge,[1] all of stone and of the color of iron, as is the circular wall that environs it. Right in the middle of this malign field yawns a very wide and deep pit, the structure of which I will tell of in its place. That belt, therefore, which remains between the pit and the foot of the high hard bank is circular, and it has its bed divided into ten valleys. Such a figure as where, for guard of the walls, very many moats encircle castles, the place where they are presents, such image did these make here. And as in such strongholds from their thresholds to the outer bank are little bridges, so from the base of the cliff ran crags which traversed the embankments and the moats far as the pit which cuts them off and collects them.

In this place we found ourselves, shaken off from the back of Geryon; and the Poet held to the left, and I moved on behind. On the right hand I saw new woe, new torments, and new scourgers, with which the first pouch was replete. At its bottom were the sinners naked; on this side the middle they came facing us; on the further side along with us, but with greater steps. As the Romans, because of the great host in the year of the Jubilee,[2] have taken means for the passage of the people over the bridge, so that on one side all have their front toward the Castle, and go to Saint Peter's, and on the other rim toward the Mount.

Along the gloomy rock, on this side and on that, I saw horned demons with great whips, who were beating them cruelly from behind. Ah, how they made them lift their heels at the first blows! truly not one waited for the second, or the third.

While I was going on, my eyes were encountered by one, and I said straightway thus: "Ere now for sight of him I have not fasted;" wherefore to shape him out I stayed my feet, and the sweet Leader stopped with me, and assented to my going somewhat back. And that scourged one thought to conceal himself by lowering his face, but it availed him little, for I said: "Thou that castest thine eye upon the ground, if the features that thou bearest are not false, art Venedico Caccianimico; but what brings thee to such stinging Salse?"

And he to me: "Unwillingly I tell it, but thy plain

speech compels me, which makes me remember the old world. I was he who brought the beautiful Ghisola[3] to do the will of the Marquis, however the shameful tale may be reported. And not the only Bolognese do I weep here; nay, this place is so full of them, that so many tongues are not now taught between Savena and the Reno to say *sipa;* and if of this thou wishest assurance or testimony, bring to mind our avaricious breasts." As he spoke thus a demon struck him with his thong and said: "Begone, pander, here are no women for coining."

I rejoined my Escort; then with few steps we came to where a crag jutted from the bank. We ascended it easily enough, and turning to the right upon its ridge, from those eternal encircling walls we departed.

When we were there where it opens[4] below to give passage to the scourged, the Leader said: "Wait, and let the sight strike on thee of these others born to ill, of whom thou hast not yet seen the face, because they have gone along together with us."

From the old bridge we looked at the train that was coming toward us on the other side, and which the scourge in like manner drives on. The good Master, without my asking, said to me: "Look at that great one who is coming, and seems not to shed a tear for pain. What royal aspect he still retains! He is Jason, who by courage and by wit despoiled the Colchians of their ram. He passed by the isle of Lemnos, after the bold pitiless women had given all their males to death. There with tokens and with ornate words he deceived Hypsipyle, the maiden, who first had deceived all the others. There he left her big with child, and lonely; such guilt condemns him to such torment; and also for Medea is vengeance wrought. With him goes whoever in such wise deceives. And let this suffice to know of the first valley, and of those that it holds in its fangs."

We were now where the narrow path intersects with the second embankment, and makes of that abutments for another arch. From there we heard people whining in the next pouch, and puffing with their muzzles, and beating themselves with their palms. The banks were encrusted with a mould by the breath from below which sticks on them, and was making quarrel with the eyes and with the nose. The bottom is so hollowed out that no place suffices us for seeing it, without mounting to the crown of the arch where the crag rises highest. Hither we came, and thence I saw down in the ditch people plunged in a filth that seemed to have come from human privies.

And while I am searching down there with my eye, I saw one with his head so foul with ordure that it was not apparent whether he were layman or clerk. He shouted to me: "Why art thou so greedy to look more at me than at the other filthy ones?" And I to him: "Because, if I remember rightly, ere now I have seen thee with dry hair, and thou art Alessio Interminei of Lucca; therefore I eye thee more than all the rest." And he then, beating his pate: "Down here the flatteries wherewith I never had my tongue cloyed have submerged me."

Hereupon my Leader said to me: "Mind thou push thy look a little further forwards so that thou mayest quite reach with thine eyes the face of that dirty and disheveled wench, who is scratching herself there with her nasty nails, and now is crouching down and now standing on foot. She is Thais the harlot, who answered her paramour when he said: 'Have I great thanks from thee?'—'Nay, marvelous.' And herewith let our sight be satisfied."

Canto XIX

Eighth Circle: third pouch: simonists.—Pope Nicholas III.

O SIMON MAGUS[1] O wretched followers, because ye, rapacious, do prostitute for gold and silver the things of God which ought to be the brides of righteousness, now it behoves for you the trumpet sound, since ye are in the third pouch.

We were now at the next tomb, having mounted on that part of the crag which hangs plumb just over the middle of the ditch. O Supreme Wisdom, how great is the art which Thou dost display in heaven, on earth, and in the evil world! and how justly does Thy Power apportion!

Upon the sides and upon the bottom, I saw the livid stone full of holes all of one size, and each was circular. They seemed to me not less wide nor larger than those that in my beautiful Saint John are made for place of the baptizers; one of which, not many years ago, I broke for the sake of one who was stifling in it: and let this be the seal to undeceive all men.

Forth from the mouth of each were protruding the feet of a sinner, and his legs up to the calf, and the rest was within. Both the soles of all of them were on fire, because of which their joints were twitching so hard that they would have snapped ropes and withes. As the flaming of things oiled is wont to move only on the outer surface, so was it there from the heels to the toes.

"Who is he, Master, who torments himself, twitching more than the others his consorts," said I, "and whom a ruddier flame is sucking?" And he to me: "If thou wilt that I carry thee down there by that bank which is the more sloping, from him thou shalt know of himself and of his wrongs." And I: "Whatever pleases thee is to my liking: thou art Lord, and knowest that I part me not from thy will, and thou knowest that which is unspoken."

Then we went upon the fourth embankment, turned, and descended on the left hand, down to the bottom pierced with holes, and narrow. The good Master set me not yet down from his haunch, till he brought me to the cleft of him who was thus lamenting with his shanks.

"O wretched soul, whoso thou art, that keepest upside down, planted like a stake," I began to say, "say a word, if thou canst." I was standing like the friar who confesses the perfidious assassin,[2] who, after he is fixed, recalls him, in order to delay his death.

And he[3] cried out: "Art thou already standing

there? Art thou already standing there, Boniface? By several years the writing lied to me. Art thou so quickly sated with that having, for which thou didst not fear to seize by guile the beautiful Lady,[4] and then to do her outrage?"

Such I became as those who, through not comprehending that which is replied to them, stand as if mocked, and know not what to answer.

Then Virgil said: "Tell him quickly, I am not he, I am not he that thou thinkest." And I answered as was enjoined on me; whereat the spirit writhed violently both his feet; then, sighing and with tearful voice, he said to me: "What then dost thou want of me? If to know who I am concern thee so much that thou hast therefore come down the bank, know that I was vested with the Great Mantle: and verily I was a son of the She-Bear,[5] so eager to advance the cubs, that up there I put wealth, and here myself, into the purse. Beneath my head are the others that preceded me in simony, dragged down flattened through the fissures of the rock. Down there shall I in my turn sink, when he shall come whom I believed that thou wast, then when I put my sudden question; but already the time is longer that I have cooked my feet, and that I have been thus upside down, than he will stay planted with his feet red; for after him will come from westward, a shepherd without law, of uglier deed, such as befits to cover him and me. A new Jason will he be, of whom it is read in Maccabees; and as to that one his king was compliant, so to this one he who rules France shall be."

I know not if here I was too foolhardy that I answered him only in this strain: "Pray now tell me, how much treasure did our Lord require of Saint Peter before he placed the keys in his keeping? Surely he asked nothing save: 'Follow thou me.'[6] Nor did Peter or the others take gold or silver of Matthias, when he was chosen by lot to the place which the guilty soul had lost. Therefore stay thou, for thou art rightly punished, and guard well the ill-gotten money that made thee bold against Charles. And were it not that reverence for the supreme keys which thou heldest in the glad life even now forbids it to me, I would use still heavier words; for your avarice afflicts the world, trampling down the good and exalting the bad. Ye shepherds the Evangelist had in mind, when she that sitteth upon the waters was seen by him to fornicate with kings: she that was born with the seven heads, and from the ten horns had argument, so long as virtue pleased her spouse. Ye have made you a god of gold and silver: and what else is there between you and the idolaters save that they worship one, and ye a hundred? Ah Constantine! of how much ill was mother, not thy conversion, but that dowry which the first rich Father took from thee!"[7]

And, while I was singing these notes to him, whether anger or conscience stung him, he was kicking hard with both his feet. I believe, indeed, that it pleased my Leader, with so contented look did he all the while give heed to the sound of the true words uttered. Thereupon with both his arms he took me, and when he had me wholly on his breast, remounted along the way whereby he had descended. Nor did he tire of holding me clasped to him, till he had thus borne me up to the top of the arch which is the passage from the fourth to the fifth embankment. Here he gently laid down his burden, gently because of the rugged and steep crag, which would be a difficult pass for goats. Thence another great valley was discovered to me.

CANTO XX

*Eighth Circle: fourth pouch: diviners, soothsay-
ers, and magicians.—Amphiaraus.—Tiresias.—
Aruns.—Manto.—Eurypylus.—Michael Scot.—
Asdente.*

OF A NEW PUNISHMENT it behoves me to make
verses, and give material to the twentieth canto of
the first lay, which is of the submerged.

I was now wholly in position to look into the uncov-
ered depth which was bathed with tears of anguish, and
I saw folk come, silent and weeping, along the great cir-
cular valley, at the pace which the litanies make in this
world. As my sight descended lower on them each ap-
peared marvelously distorted between the chin and the
beginning of the chest; for their face was turned toward
their reins, and they must needs go backwards, because
looking forward was taken from them. Perhaps indeed

by force of palsy some one has been thus completely twisted, but I never saw it, nor do I believe it can be.

So may God let thee, Reader, gather fruit from thy reading, now think for thyself how I could keep my face dry, when close at hand I saw our image so contorted that the weeping of the eyes bathed the buttocks along the cleft. Truly I wept, leaning on one of the rocks of the hard crag, so that my Guide said to me: "Art thou even yet among the other fools? Here pity lives when it is quite dead.[1] Who is more criminal than he who brings passion to the Divine Judgment? Lift up thy head, lift up, and see him for whom the earth opened before the eyes of the Thebans, whereat they all shouted: 'Whither art thou rushing, Amphiaraus? Why dost thou leave the war?' And he stopped not from falling headlong down far as Minos, who lays hold on every one. Look, how he has made a breast of his shoulders! Because he wished to see too far before him, he looks behind and goes a backward path.

"Behold Tiresias,[2] who changed semblance, when from male he became female, transforming all his members; and afterwards he was obliged to strike again with his rod the two entwined serpents, ere he could regain his masculine plumage. He who has his back to this one's belly is Aruns, who on the mountains of Luni (where grubs the man of Carrara who dwells below) had a cave for his abode among white marbles, whence for looking at the stars and the sea his view was not cut off.

"And she who with her loose tresses covers her breasts, which thou dost not see, and has on that side all her hairy skin, was Manto,[3] who roamed through many lands, then settled there where I was born; whereof it pleases me that thou listen a little to me. After her father had departed from life, and the city of Bacchus[4] had become enslaved, she wandered long while through the world. Up in fair Italy, at foot of the alp which shuts in Germany above Tyrol, lies a lake which is called Benaco. By a thousand founts, I think, and more, between Garda and Val Camonica, Apennino is bathed by the water which settles in that lake. A place is in the middle there, where the Trentine Pastor and he of Brescia and the Veronese might each give his blessing if he took that road. Peschiera, a fair and strong fortress, to front the Brescians and Bergamasques, sits where the shore round about is lowest. There that which in the bosom of Benaco cannot stay must needs all pour forth, and it becomes a river down through green pastures. Soon as the water gathers head to run, it is no longer called Benaco, but Mincio, far as Governo, where it falls into the Po. It has no long course before it finds a flat, on which it spreads, and makes a marsh, and is apt at times in summer to be noisome. Passing that way, the savage virgin saw land in the middle of the fen, without culture and bare of inhabitants. There, to avoid all human fellowship, she stayed with her servants to practice her arts, and lived, and left there her body empty. Afterward the men who were scattered round about gathered to that place, which was strong because of the fen which it had on all sides. They built the city over those dead bones, and for her, who first had chosen the place, they called it Mantua, without other augury. Formerly its people were more thick within it, before the stupidity of Casalodi had been tricked by Pinamonte. Therefore I instruct thee that if thou ever hearest that my city had other origin, no falsehood may defraud the truth."

And I: "Master, thy discourses are so certain to me, and so lay hold on my faith, that the others would be to me as spent coals. But tell me of the people who are going onward, if thou seest any one of them worthy of note; for only to that does my mind revert."

Then he said to me: "That one, who stretches his beard from his cheek over his dusky shoulders, was an augur when Greece was so emptied of males that they scarcely remained for the cradles, and with Calchas he gave the moment for cutting the first cable at Aulis. Eurypylus[5] was his name, and thus my lofty Tragedy sings him in some place; well thou knowest this, who knowest the whole of it. That other who is so spare in the flanks was Michael Scot, who verily knew the game of magical deceptions. Behold Guido Bonatti, behold Asdente, who now would wish he had attended to his leather and his thread, but too late repents. Behold the wretched women who left the needle, the spool, and the spindle, and became fortune-tellers; they wrought spells with herbs and with image.

"But come on now, for already Cain with his thorns[6] holds the confines of both the hemispheres, and touches the wave below Seville; and already yesternight was the moon round; well shouldst thou remember it, for it did thee no harm sometimes in the deep wood." Thus he spoke to me, and we went on the while.

Canto XXI

Eighth Circle: fifth pouch: barrators.—A magistrate of Lucca.—The Malebranche.—Parley with them.

Thus from bridge to bridge we went, talking of other things, which my Comedy cares not to sing, and were holding the summit, when we stopped to see the next cleft of Malebolge and the next vain lamentations; and I saw it wonderfully dark.

As in the Arsenal of the Venetians, in winter, the sticky pitch for paying their unsound vessels is boiling, because they cannot sail the sea, and, instead thereof, one builds him a new bark, and one caulks the ribs of that which has made many a voyage; one hammers at the prow, and one at the stern; another makes oars, and another twists cordage; and one patches the foresail and the mainsail,—so, not by fire, but by divine art, a thick pitch was boiling there below, which belimed the bank on every side. I saw it, but saw not in it aught but the bubbles which the boiling raised, and all of it swelling up and again settling down compressed.

While I was gazing down there fixedly, my Leader, saying: "Beware! beware! " drew me to himself from the place where I was standing. Then I turned as one who is in haste to see that from which it behoves him to fly, and whom a sudden fear dismays, and who for seeing delays not to depart, and I saw behind us a black devil come running up along the crag. Ah! how fell he was in aspect, and how bitter he seemed to me in act, with his wings open, and light upon his feet! His shoulder, which was sharp and high, was laden by a sinner with both haunches, the sinews of whose feet he held clutched. "O Malebranche[1] of our bridge," he said, "lo here, one of the Ancients of Saint Zita! put him under, for I am returning for still others to that city, which I have furnished well with them; every man there is a barrator,[2] except Bonturo: there, for money, out of Nay is made Ay." Down he hurled him and turned back along the hard crag, and never mastiff loosed was in such haste to follow a thief.

That one sank under, and rose again doubled up, but the demons that had cover of the bridge cried out: "Here the Holy Face has no place; here one swims otherwise than in the Serchio; therefore, if thou dost not want our grapples, make no show above the pitch." Then they pricked him with more than a hundred prongs, and said: "Here thou must dance under cover, so that, if thou canst, thou mayst swindle secretly." Not otherwise do the cooks make their scullions plunge the meat with their hooks into the middle of the cauldron, so that it may not float.

The good Master said to me: "In order that it be not apparent that thou art here, squat down behind a jag that thou mayst have some screen for thyself, and at any offence that may be done to me be not afraid, for I have knowledge of these things, because once before I was in such a wrangle."

Then he passed on beyond the head of the bridge, and when he arrived upon the sixth bank, he had need to have a steadfast front. With that fury and with that storm, with which dogs run out upon the poor wretch, who where he stops suddenly asks alms, they came forth from under the little bridge, and turned against him all their grapples. But he cried out: "Let no one of you be savage; before your hook take hold of me, let one of you come forward that he may hear me, and then take counsel as to grappling me." All cried out "Let Malacoda[3] go;" whereon, while the rest stood still, one moved and came to him, saying: "What does this profit him?" "Thinkest thou, Malacoda, to see me come here," said my Master, "safe hitherto from all your hindrances, except by Divine Will and propitious fate? Let me go on, for in Heaven it is willed that I show to another this wild road." Then was his arrogance so fallen that he let the hook drop at his feet, and said to the others: "Now he may not be struck."

And my Leader to me: "O thou that sittest asquat among the splinters of the bridge, return now securely to me." Wherefore I moved and came swiftly to him; and the devils all pressed forward, so that I feared they would not keep compact. And thus I once

saw the foot-soldiers afraid, who were coming out
from Caprona under pledge, seeing themselves
among so many enemies. I drew close with my whole
body to my Leader's side, and did not turn my eyes
from their look, which was not good. They were low-
ering their forks, and one was saying to the other:
"Wilt thou that I touch him on the rump? " and they
were answering: "Yes, see that thou nick it for him."
But that demon who was holding speech with my
Leader turned round with all haste and said : "Quiet,
quiet, Scarmiglione!"

Then he said to us: "Further advance along this
crag is not possible, because the sixth arch lies all
shattered at the bottom. And if it be still your plea-
sure to go forward, go on along this ridge; near by is
another crag that affords a way. Yesterday, five hours
later than this, completed one thousand two hundred
and sixty-six years since the way was broken here.[4] I
am sending thitherward some of these of mine, to
see if any one is airing himself; go ye with them, for
they will not be wicked. Come forward, Alichino and
Calcabrina," he began to say, "and thou, Cagnazzo;
and Barbariccia, do thou guide the ten. Let Libi-
cocco go also, and Draghignazzo, tusked Ciriatto,
and Graffiacane, and Farfarello, and mad Rubi-
cante.[5] Search round about the boiling pitch; let
these be safe far as the next crag, which all unbroken
goes over these dens."

"O me! Master, what is this that I see?" said I; "pray,
if thou knowest the way, let us go alone without escort,
for as for myself I crave it not. If thou art as wary as thou
art wont, dost thou not see that they grin, and with their

brows threaten harm to us?" And he to me: " I would
not have thee afraid; let them grin on at their will, for
they are doing it at the boiled sufferers."

Upon the left bank they took a turn, but first each
had pressed his tongue with his teeth toward their
leader as a signal, and he had made a trumpet of his
rump.

CANTO XXII

Eighth Circle: fifth pouch, continued: barrators.—Ciampolo of Navarre.—Fra Gomita.—Michael Zanche.—Fray of the Malebranche.

I HAVE SEEN ERE now horsemen moving camp, and beginning an assault, and making their muster, and sometimes retiring for their escape; I have seen foragers over your land, O Aretines, and I have seen the starting of raids, the onset of tournaments, and the running of jousts, now with trumpets, and now with bells, with drums, and with signals from strongholds, and with native things and foreign,—but never to so strange a pipe did I see horsemen or footmen set forth, or ship by sign of land or star.

We were going along with the ten demons. Ah, the fell company! but in the church with the saints, and in the tavern with the gluttons. My attention was only on the pitch in order to see every condition of the pouch, and of the people that were burning in it.

Like dolphins, when by the arching of their back, they give a sign to the sailors to take heed for the safety of their vessel, so, now and then, to alleviate his pain, one of the sinners would show his back and hide it in less time than it lightens. And as at the edge of the water of a ditch the frogs lie with only their muzzle out, so that they conceal their feet and the rest of their bulk, so on every side were the sinners; but as Barbariccia approached so did they draw back beneath the boiling. I saw, and still my heart shudders at it, one waiting, just as it happens that one frog stays and another jumps. And Graffiacane, who was nearest over against him, hooked him by his pitchy locks, and drew him up so that he seemed to me an otter. (I knew now the name of every one of them, I had so noted them when they were chosen, and afterwards when they called each other had listened how.) "O Rubicante, see thou set thy claws upon his back so thou flay him," shouted all the accursed ones together.

And I: "My Master, contrive, if thou canst, to find out who is the luckless one come into the hands of his adversaries." My Leader drew up to his side, and asked him whence he was, and he replied: "I was born in the kingdom of Navarre; my mother placed me in service of a lord, for she had borne me to a ribald, destroyer of himself and of his substance. Afterward I was of the household of the good King Thibault;[1] there I set myself to practice barratry, for which I pay reckoning in this heat."

And Ciriatto, from whose mouth protruded on either side a tusk, as of a boar, made him feel how one of them rips. Among evil cats had the mouse come; but Barbariccia clasped him in his arms, and said: "Stand off, while I clutch him," and turned his face to my Master. "Ask further," said he, "if thou desirest to know more from him, before another one undo him." The Leader: "Then, tell now of the other sinners; knowest thou any one under the pitch who is Italian?" And he: "I parted short while since from one who there beyond was a neighbor; would that with him I still were so covered that I should not fear claw or hook." And Libicocco said: "We have borne too much," and seized his arm with his grapple so that, tearing, he carried off a sinew of it. Draghignazzo, he too wished to give him a grip down at his legs, whereat their decurion turned round about with evil look.

When they were a little quieted, my Leader, without delay, asked him who was still gazing at his wound: "Who was he from whom thou sayst thou madest ill parting to come to shore?" And he replied: "It was Friar Gomita, he of Gallura, vessel of every fraud, who held the enemies of his lord in hand, and dealt so with them that each of them praises him for it. Money he took, and let them smoothly off, so he says; and in his other offices besides he was no little barrator, but sovereign. With him frequents Don Michael Zanche of Logodoro, and their tongues never feel tired in talking of Sardinia. O me! see ye that other who is grinning: I would say more, but I fear lest he is making ready to scratch my itch." And the grand Provost, turning to Farfarello, who was rolling his eyes as if to strike, said: "Get away there, wicked bird!"

"If ye wish to see or to hear Tuscans or Lombards," thereon began again the frightened one, "I will make some of them come; but let the Malebranche stand a little withdrawn, so that they may not be afraid of their vengeance, and I, sitting in this very place, for one that I am, will make seven of them come, when I shall whistle, as is our wont to do whenever one of us sets himself outside." Cagnazzo at this speech raised his muzzle, shaking his head, and said: "Hear the cunning trick he has devised for casting himself below!" Whereon he who had snares in great plenty answered: "Too cunning am I when I procure for my own companions greater sorrow." Alichino held not in, and, in opposition to the others, said to him: "If thou plunge, I will not come after thee at a gallop, but I will beat my wings above the pitch; let the ridge be left, and let the bank be a screen, to see if thou alone availest more than we."

O thou that readest, thou shalt hear a new sport! Each turned his eyes to the other side, he first who had been most averse to doing this. The Navarrese chose his time well, planted his feet firmly on the ground, and in an instant leaped, and from their purpose freed himself. At this, each of them was stung with his fault, but he most who was the cause of the loss; wherefore he started and cried out: "Thou art caught." But it availed little, for wings could not outstrip fear. The one went under, and the other, flying, turned his breast upward. Not otherwise the wild duck on a sudden dives under when the falcon comes near, and he returns up vexed and baffled. Calcabrina, angry at the flout, flying kept behind him, charmed that the sinner should escape, that he might have a scuffle; and when the barrator had disappeared he at once turned his claws upon his companion, and grappled with him above the ditch. But the other was indeed a full-grown sparrowhawk for clawing him well, and both of them fell into the middle of the boiling pool. The heat was a sudden ungrappler; but yet there was no rising from it, they had their wings so beglued. Barbariccia, in distress with the others of his troop, made four of them fly to the other side with all their forks, and very swiftly, on this side and that, they descended to their posts, and stretched their hooks toward the belimed ones, who were already cooked within the crust: and we left them thus embroiled.

Canto XXIII

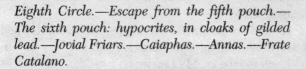

*Eighth Circle.—Escape from the fifth pouch.—
The sixth pouch: hypocrites, in cloaks of gilded
lead.—Jovial Friars.—Caiaphas.—Annas.—Frate
Catalano.*

Silent, alone, and without company, we were going
on, one before, the other behind, as Minor friars go
along the way. My thought was turned by the present
brawl upon the fable of Aesop, in which he told of the
frog and the mouse; for *now* and *this instant* are not
more alike than the one is to the other, if beginning and
end be rightly coupled by the attentive mind. And as
one thought bursts out from another, so then from that
was born another which made my first fear double. I
was thinking in this wise: These through us have been
put to scorn, and with such harm and trick as I believe
must vex them greatly; if anger be added to ill-will, they

will come after us more merciless than the dog to the hare which he snaps up.

Already I was feeling my hair all bristling with fear, and was backwards intent, when I said: "Master, if thou dost not speedily conceal thyself and me, I am afraid of the Malebranche; we have them already after us; I so imagine them that I already feel them." And he: "If I were of leaded glass,[1] I should not draw to me thine outward image more quickly than I receive thine inward. Even now came thy thoughts among mine, with like action and like look, so that of both I made one sole counsel. If it be that the right bank lies so that we can descend into the next pouch, we shall escape from the imagined chase."

He had not yet finished reporting this counsel, when I saw them coming with wings spread, not very far off, with will to take us. My Leader on a sudden took me, as a mother who is wakened by the noise, and sees the kindled flames close to her, who takes her son and flies, and, having more care of him than of herself, stays not so long as only to put on a shift: and down from the ridge of the hard bank, he gave himself supine to the sloping rock that closes one of the sides of the next pouch. Never ran water so swiftly through a duct, to turn the wheel of a land-mill, when it approaches nearest to the paddles, as my Master over that border, bearing me along upon his breast as his son and not as a companion. Hardly had his feet reached the bed of the depth below, when they were on the ridge right over us; but here there was no fear, for the high Providence that willed to set them as ministers of the fifth ditch deprived them all of power of departing thence.

There below we found a painted people who were going round with very slow steps, weeping, and in their semblance weary and subdued. They had cloaks, with hoods lowered before their eyes, fashioned of the cut which is made for the monks in Cologne. Outwardly they are gilded, so that it dazzles, but within all lead, and so heavy that those Frederick used to have put on were of straw.[2] O mantle wearisome for eternity!

We turned, still ever to the left hand, along with them, intent on their sad plaint. But because of the weight, that tired folk were coming so slowly that we had fresh company at every movement of the haunch. Wherefore I to my Leader: "Contrive to find some one who may be known by deed or name, and while thus going move thine eyes around." And one who heard the Tuscan speech cried out behind us: "Stay your feet, ye who run thus through the dusky air; perchance thou shalt have from me that which thou askest." Whereon my Leader turned and said: "Wait, and then proceed according to his pace." I stopped, and saw two show, by their look, great haste of mind to be with me, but their load and the narrow way retarded them.

When they had come up, awhile, with eye askance,[3] they gazed at me without speaking a word; then they turned to one another, and said one to the other: "This one seems alive by the action of his throat; and if they are dead, by what privilege do they go uncovered by the heavy stole?" Then they said to me: "O Tuscan, who to the college of the wretched hypocrites art come, hold it not in disdain to tell who thou art." And I to them: "I was born and grew up on the fair river of Arno, at the great town, and I am in the body that I have always had.

But who are ye, from whom such woe distils, as I see, down along your cheeks? and what penalty is it that so glitters on you?" And one of them replied to me: "The orange hoods are of lead so thick that the weights thus make their scales to creak.[4] Jovial Friars were we, and Bolognese; I named Catalano and he Loderingo, and together taken by thy city, as one man alone is usually chosen, in order to preserve its peace: and we were such as still is apparent round about the Gardingo." I began: "O Friars, your ills"—but more I said not, for there struck my eye one crucified upon the ground with three stakes. When he saw me he writhed all over, blowing into his beard with sighs: and the Friar Catalano, who observed it, said to me: "That transfixed one, whom thou lookest at, counseled the Pharisees that it was expedient to put one man to torture for the people. Traverse and naked is he on the path, as thou seest, and he first must needs feel how much whoever passes weighs.[5] And in like fashion his father-in-law is stretched in this ditch, and the others of that Council which for the Jews was seed of ill." Then I saw Virgil marvel[6] over him that was outstretched in a cross so vilely in the eternal exile. Afterwards he addressed this speech to the Friar: "May it not displease you, if it be allowed you, to tell us if any opening lies on the right hand, whereby we two can go out hence without constraining any of the Black Angels to come to deliver us from this deep." He answered then: "Nearer than thou hopest is a rock that starts from the great encircling wall and spans all the savage valleys, save that at this one it is broken, and does not cover it. Ye will be able to mount up over the ruin that lies against the side, and heaps up at the bottom." My Leader stood a little while with bowed head, then said: "Ill did he who hooks the sinners yonder report the matter." And the Friar: "Of old at Bologna I used to hear tell of vices enough of the devil, among which I heard that he is a liar, and the father of falsehood." Then my Leader went on, with great steps, disturbed a little with anger in his look; whereon I departed from the burdened ones, following the prints of the beloved feet.

CANTO XXIV

Eighth Circle. The poets climb from the sixth pouch.—Seventh pouch filled with serpents, by which thieves are tormented.—Vanni Fucci.—Prophecy of calamity to Dante.

IN THAT PART of the young year when the sun tempers his locks beneath Aquarius,¹ and now the nights are passing to the South, when the hoar frost copies on the ground the image of her white sister, but the temper of her pen lasts little while, the rustic, whose provision fails, gets up and looks, and sees the plain all white, whereat he smites his thigh, returns indoors, and grumbles to and fro, like the poor wretch who knows not what to do; then goes out again and picks up hope, seeing the world to have changed face in short while, and takes his crook and drives forth his sheep to pasture. Thus my Master made me dismayed, when I saw his

brow so disturbed, and thus speedily arrived the plaster
for the hurt. For when we came to the ruined bridge,
the Leader turned to me with that sweet look which I
first saw at the foot of the mount. After taking some
counsel with himself, looking first well at the ruin, he
opened his arms, and laid hold of me. And as one who
acts and considers, and seems always to provide in ad-
vance, so, lifting me up toward the top of a great rock,
he was taking note of another splinter, saying: "Grapple
next on that, but try first if it be such that it can support
thee." It was no way for one clothed in a cloak, for we
with difficulty, he light and I pushed up, could mount
from jag to jag. And had it not been that on that
precinct the bank was shorter than on the other side, I
do not know about him, but I should have been com-
pletely vanquished. But because all Malebolge slopes
toward the opening of the lowest well, the site of each
valley imports that one side is higher than the other. We
came, however, at length, to the point where the last
stone is broken off. The breath was so milked from my
lungs when I was up that I could no farther, nay, sat me
down on first arrival.

"Henceforth it behoves thee thus[2] to put off sloth,"
said the Master, "for, sitting upon down or under quilts,
one comes not to fame, without which he who con-
sumes his life leaves such vestige of himself on earth as
smoke in air, or the foam on water: and therefore rise
up, conquer thy panting with the soul that wins every
battle, if it be not weighed down by its heavy body. A
longer stairway needs must be ascended: it is not
enough to have departed from these; if thou under-
standest me, now act so that it avail thee." Then I rose

up, showing myself better furnished with breath than I felt, and said: "Go on, for I am strong and resolute."

Up along the crag we took the way, which was rugged, narrow, and difficult, and far steeper than the one before. I was going along speaking in order not to seem exhausted, when a voice, ill suited for forming words, came out from the next ditch. I know not what it said, though I was already upon the back of the arch which crosses here; but he who was speaking seemed moved to anger. I had turned downwards, but my living eyes could not go to the bottom, through the darkness: wherefore I said: "Master, see that thou get to the next girth, and let us descend the wall, for as from this place I hear and do not understand, so I look down and shape out nothing." "Other reply," he said, "I give thee not than the doing, for the becoming request ought to be followed by the deed in silence."

We descended the bridge at its head, where it is joined with the eighth bank, and then the pouch was apparent to me. And I saw within it a terrible crowd of serpents, and of such strange kind that the memory still curdles my blood. Let Libya with her sand vaunt herself no more; for though she bring forth chelydri, jaculi, and phareae, and cenchri with amphisboena[3] she never, with all Ethiopia, nor with the land that lies on the Red Sea, showed either so many or so malignant plagues.

Amid this cruel and most dismal swarm were running people naked and terrified, without hope of hole or heliotrope.[4] They had their hands tied behind with serpents, which fixed their tail and their head through the loins, and were twisted up in front.

And lo! at one, who was near our bank, darted a serpent that transfixed him there where the neck is knotted to the shoulders. Nor *O* nor *I* was ever so quickly written as he took fire and burnt, and needs must become all ashes as he fell; and when he was thus destroyed on the ground, the dust drew together of itself, and in an instant into that same one returned. Thus by the great sages it is affirmed that the Phoenix dies, and then is born again when she draws nigh to her five-hundredth year. In her life she feeds not on herb or grain, but only on tears of incense and amomum; and nard and myrrh are her last winding-sheet.

And as he who falls, and knows not how, by force of a demon that drags him to ground, or of other obstruction that binds the man when he rises and gazes around him, all bewildered by the great anguish that he has suffered, and as he looks, sighs; such was that sinner after he had risen. Oh power of God! how severe it is, that showers down such blows for vengeance!

My Leader then asked him who he was; whereon he answered: "I rained down from Tuscany short time ago into this fell gullet. Bestial life, and not human, pleased me, like a mule that I was.⁵ I am Vanni Fucci, beast, and Pistoia was my fitting den." And I to my Leader: "Tell him not to slip away, and ask what sin thrust him down here, for I have seen him a man of blood and of rages." And the sinner who heard did not dissemble, but directed toward me his mind and his face, and painted himself with dismal shame. Then he said: "It grieves me more, that thou hast caught me in the misery where thou seest me, than when I was taken from the other life. I cannot refuse that which thou askest. I am put so far down because I was the thief in the sac-

risty with the fair adornments, and it was once falsely
ascribed to another. But in order that thou enjoy not
this sight, if ever thou shalt be forth of these dark
places, open thine ears to my announcement, and hear:
Pistoia first strips herself of Blacks, then Florence reno-
vates her people and her fashions. Mars draws a vapor
from Val di Magra which is wrapt in turbid clouds, and
with impetuous and bitter storm there shall be fighting
on the Pescian plain, whence it shall suddenly rend the
mist, so that every White shall be smitten by it. And this
I have said in order that it may grieve thee."

CANTO XXV

❦

Eighth Circle: seventh pouch: fraudulent thieves.—Cacus.—Agnello Brunelleschi and others.

A T THE END of his words the thief raised his hands with both the figs,[1] crying, "Take that, God! for at Thee I square them." From that time forth the serpents were my friends, for then one coiled about his neck, as if it said: "I will not have thee say more;" and another about his arms and bound him up anew, clinching itself so in front that he could not give a shake with them. Ah Pistoia! Pistoia! why dost thou not decree to make ashes of thyself, so that thou last no longer, since in evil-doing thou dost surpass thine own seed? Through all the dark circles of Hell I saw no spirit so arrogant toward God, not even that one who fell down from the walls at Thebes. He fled away, and spoke not a word more.

And I saw a Centaur full of rage come crying out:

"Where is he, where is the obdurate one?" I do not believe Maremma² has so many snakes as he had upon his croup up to where our semblance begins. On his shoulders, behind the nape, a dragon with open wings was lying upon him, which sets on fire whomsoever it encounters. My Master said: "This is Cacus, who beneath the rock of Mount Aventine often made a lake of blood. He goes not on one road with his brothers, because of the fraudulent theft he committed of the great herd that he had in his neighborhood; for which his crooked deeds ceased under the club of Hercules, who perhaps dealt him a hundred blows with it, and he felt not ten of them."

While he was thus speaking, and that one had run by, lo! three spirits came below us, of whom neither I nor my Leader was aware till when they cried out: "Who are ye?" by which our story was stopped, and we then gave heed only to them. I did not know them, but it happened, as it usually happens by some chance, that one had occasion to name another, saying: "Where can Cianfa have stayed?" Wherefore I, in order that my Leader might be attentive, put my finger upward from my chin to my nose.

If, Reader, thou art now slow to credit that which I shall tell, it will be no marvel, for I who saw it hardly admit it to myself. As I was holding my eyebrows raised upon them, lo! a serpent with six feet darts in front of one, and takes hold all over him. With its middle feet it clasped his paunch, and with its fore feet took his arms, then struck its teeth in one and the other cheek; its hind feet it spread out upon his thighs, and put its tail between them, and stretched it up behind along the reins. Ivy was never so bearded to a tree, as the horrible beast entwined its own through the other's limbs. Then they stuck together as if they had been of hot wax, and mingled their color; neither the one nor the other seemed now that which it had been; even as in advance of the flame, a dark color proceeds up along the paper which is not yet black, and the white dies away. The other two were looking on, and each cried: "O me! Agnèl, how thou changest! See, now thou art neither two nor one!" Now were the two heads become one, when there appeared to us two countenances mixed in one face wherein the two were lost. The two arms were made of four strips; the thighs with the legs, the belly and the chest became members that were never seen before. Every original aspect was there canceled; two and none the perverted image appeared, and such it went away with slow step.

As the lizard under the great scourge of the dog-days, changing from hedge to hedge, seems a lightning-flash, if it cross the way, so seemed, coining toward the bellies of the two others, a little fiery serpent, livid, and black as a pepper corn. And it transfixed in one of them that part whereat our nourishment is first taken,[3] then fell down stretched out before him. The transfixed one gazed at it, but said nothing; nay, with feet fixed, he began to yawn, just as if sleep or fever had assailed him. He looked at the serpent, and that at him; one through the wound, the other through its mouth, were smoking fiercely, and the smoke commingled. Let Lucan henceforth be silent, where he tells of the wretched Sabellus and of Nasidius,[4] and let him wait to hear that which now is related. Let Ovid be silent concerning Cadmus

and Arethusa for if, poetizing, he converts him into a
serpent and her into a fountain, I grudge it not to him;
for never did he transmute two natures front to front,
so that both the forms were prompt to exchange their
matter. They responded to one another in such wise,
that the serpent cleft his tail into a fork, and the
wounded one drew his feet together.[5] The legs and the
thighs along with them so stuck together, that in short
while the juncture made no mark that was apparent.
The cleft tail was taking on the shape that the other was
losing, and its skin was becoming soft, and that of the
other hard. I saw the arms entering through the
armpits, and the two feet of the beast, which were
short, lengthening out in proportion as the arms were
shortening. Then the hinder feet, twisted together, be-
came the member that man conceals, and the wretch
from his had two stretched forth.[6]

While the smoke veils the one and the other with a
new color, and generates hair on the one part, and
strips it from the other, the one rose up, and the other
fell down, not however turning aside their pitiless
lights, beneath which each was changing his muzzle.
He who was erect drew his in toward the temples, and,
from the too much material that came in there, the ears
issued on the smooth cheeks; that which did not run
back and was retained, of its superfluity made a nose
for the face, and thickened the lips so much as was
needful. He that was lying down drives his muzzle for-
ward, and draws backward his ears into his head, as the
snail does its horns. And his tongue, which before was
united and fit for speech, cleaves itself, and the forked
one of the other closes up; and the smoke stops. The

soul that had become a brute fled hissing along the valley, and the other, speaking, sputters behind it. Then he turned on him his new shoulders, and said to the third, "I want that Buoso should run, as I have done, on his belly along this path."

Thus I saw the seventh ballast change and transmute, and here let the novelty be my excuse, if my pen straggle a little. And although my eyes were somewhat confused, and my mind bewildered, those could not flee away so covertly but that I clearly distinguished Puccio Sciancato: and he it was who alone, of the three companions that came first, was not changed; the other was he whom thou, Gaville, weepest.

Canto XXVI

Eighth Circle: eighth pouch: fraudulent counselors.—Ulysses and Diomed.

REJOICE, FLORENCE, since thou art so great that thou beatest thy wings over sea and land, and thy name is spread through Hell! Among the thieves I found five such, thy citizens, whereat shame comes to me, and thou dost not mount unto great honor thereby. But, if near the morning one dreams of the truth, thou shalt feel within short time what Prato, as well as others, craves for thee. And if already it were, it would not be too soon. So were it! since surely it must be; for it will weigh the more on me as the more I age.

We departed thence, and, up along the stairs which the bourns had before made for our descent, my Leader remounted and drew me. And pursuing the

solitary way among the fragments and the rocks of the
craggy bridge, the foot sped not without the hand. I
sorrowed then, and now I sorrow again when I direct
my mind to what I saw; and I curb my genius more
than I am wont, that it may not run unless virtue guide
it; so that if a good star, or better thing, have given me
the good, I may not grudge it to myself.

As many as the fireflies which, in the season when he
that brightens the world keeps his face least hidden
from us, the rustic, who is resting on the hillside what
time the fly yields to the gnat, sees down in the valley,
perhaps there where he makes his vintage and
ploughs,—with so many flames all the eighth pit was
gleaming, as I perceived so soon as I was there where
the bottom became apparent. And as he[1] who was
avenged by the bears saw the chariot of Elijah at its de-
parture, when the horses rose erect to heaven,—for he
could not so follow it with his eyes as to see aught save
the flame alone, like a little cloud, mounting upward,—
thus each of those flames was moving through the gul-
ley of the ditch, for not one shows its theft, and every
flame steals away a sinner.

I was standing on the bridge, risen up to look, so
that, if I had not taken hold of a rock, I should have
fallen below without being pushed. And my Leader,
who saw me thus intent, said: "Within these fires are
the spirits; each is swathed by that wherewith he is
burnt." "My Master," I replied, "through hearing thee
am I more certain, but already I deemed that it was
so, and already I wished to say to thee: Who is in that
fire which comes so divided at its top that it seems to
rise from the pyre on which Eteocles was put with his

brother?"[2] He answered me: "Therewithin Ulysses and Diomed are tormented, and thus they go together in their punishment, as in their wrath. And within their flame they groan for the ambush of the horse which made the gate whence the noble seed of the Romans issued forth; within it they lament the artifice whereby the dead Deidamia still mourns for Achilles, and there they bear the penalty for the Palladium."[3] "If they have power to speak within those sparks," said I, "Master, much I pray thee, and repray, that my prayer avail a thousand, that thou make not to me denial of waiting till the horned flame come hither: thou seest that with desire I bend me toward it." And he to me: "Thy prayer is worthy of much praise, and therefore I accept it; but mind that thy tongue restrain itself. Leave speech to me, for I have conceived that which thou wishest; for, because they were Greeks, they would perhaps be disdainful of thy words."

When the flame had come there where it seemed to my Leader time and place, I heard him speak to it in this form: "O ye, who are two within one fire, if I deserved of you while I lived, if I deserved of you much or little, when in the world I wrote my lofty verses, move not, but let one of you tell, whither, being lost, he went away to die." The greater horn of the ancient flame began to wag, murmuring, even as a flame that the wind wearies. Then waving its tip to and fro, as if it were the tongue that spoke, it cast forth a voice, and said:—

"When I departed from Circe, who had detained me more than a year there near to Gaeta, before Aeneas had so named it, neither fondness for my son, nor piety for my old father, nor the due love which should have made Penelope glad, could overcome within me the ardor which I had to become experienced of the world, and of the vices of men, and of their virtue. But I put forth on the deep, open sea, with one vessel only, and with that little company by which I had not been deserted. I saw one shore and the other[4] as far as Spain, as far as Morocco and the island of Sardinia, and the others which that sea bathes round about. I and my companions were old and slow when we came to that narrow strait where Hercules set up his bounds, to the end that man should not put out beyond.[5] On the right hand I left Seville, on the other I had already left Ceuta. 'O brothers,' I said, 'who through a hundred thousand perils have reached the West, to this so brief vigil of your senses which remains wish not to deny the experience, following the sun, of the world that has no people. Consider your origin; ye were not made to live as brutes, but to pursue virtue and knowledge.' With this little speech I made my companions so keen for the voyage that hardly afterwards could I have held them back. And turning our stern to the morning, with our oars we made wings for the mad flight, always gaining on the left hand side. The night saw now all the stars of the other pole, and ours so low that it rose not forth from the ocean floor. The light beneath the moon had been five times rekindled and as many quenched, since we had entered on the passage of the deep, when there appeared to us a mountain dark in the distance, and it seemed to me so high as I had never seen one. We rejoiced, and soon it turned to lamentation, for from the new land a whirlwind rose and struck the fore part of the vessel. Three times it made her whirl with all the waters, the fourth it made her stern lift up and the prow go down, as pleased Another, till the sea had closed over us."

Canto XXVII

Eighth Circle: eighth pouch: fraudulent coun-selors.—Guido da Montefeltro.

THE FLAME was already erect and quiet, by reason of not speaking more, and already was going from us, with the permission of the sweet poet, when another, which was coming behind it, made us turn our eyes to its tip, by a confused sound that was issuing forth from it. As the Sicilian bull, which bellowed first with the plaint of him (and that was right) who had shaped it with his tools, was wont to bellow with the voice of the sufferer, so that, although it was of brass, yet it appeared transfixed with the pain, so, through not at first having way or outlet from the fire, the disconsolate words were converted into its language. But when they had taken their course up through the point, giving to it in their passage that vibration which the tongue had given, we heard say: "O thou, to whom I direct my voice, and who just now wast speaking Lombard, saying: 'Now go thy way, no more I urge thee:' although I may have arrived perhaps somewhat late, let it not irk thee to stop to speak with me; behold, it irks not me, and I am burning. If thou art but now fallen into this blind world from that sweet Italian land whence I bring all my sin, tell me if the Romagnoles have peace or war; for I was of the mountains there, between Urbino and the chain from which Tiber is unlocked."

I was still downward attent and leaning over, when my Leader touched me on the side, saying, "Speak thou, this is an Italian." And I, who already had my answer ready, without delay began to speak: "O soul, that art hidden down there, thy Romagna is not, and never was, without war in the hearts of her tyrants, but no open war have I left there now. Ravenna is as it has been for many years; the eagle of Polenta is brooding there, so that he covers Cervia with his wings. The city that made some while ago the long struggle, and of the French a bloody heap, finds itself again beneath the green paws. And the old mastiff and the new of Verrucchio, who made the ill disposal of Montagna, make an auger of their teeth there where they are wont. The young lion of the white lair, who changes side from summer to winter, rules the cities of Lamone and of Santerno. And she whose flank the Savio bathes lives between tyranny and a free state, even as she sits between the plain and the mountain. Now I pray thee that thou tell us who thou art; be not harder than another has been, so may thy name hold front in the world."

After the fire had roared for a while according to its

fashion, the sharp point moved to and fro, and then gave forth this breath: "If I believed that my reply were to a person who should ever return to the world, this flame would stand without more quiverings; but inasmuch as, if I hear truth, never did any one return alive from this depth, I answer thee without fear of infamy.

"I was a man of arms, and then I was a cordelier, trusting, thus girt, to make amends; and surely my trust had come full but for the Great Priest, whom ill befall! who set me back into my first sins; and how and wherefore, I will that thou hear from me. While I was that shape of bone and flesh which my mother gave me, my works were not leonine, but of the fox. All wily practices and covert ways I knew, and I so plied their art that the sound went forth to the end of the earth. When I saw me arrived at that part of my age where every one ought to strike the sails and coil up the ropes, what before was pleasing to me then was irksome to me, and I yielded me repentant and confessed. Ah wretched, alas! and it would have availed. The Prince of the new Pharisees having war near the Lateran,—and not with Saracens nor with Jews, for every enemy of his was Christian, and not one of them had been to conquer Acre, or a trafficker in the land of the Soldan,—regarded in himself neither his supreme office, nor his Holy Orders, nor in me that cord which was wont to make those girt with it more lean; but as Constantine besought Sylvester[1] within Soracte to cure his leprosy, so this one besought me as master to cure the fever of his pride. He asked counsel of me, and I kept silence, because his words seemed drunken. And then he said to me: 'Let not thy heart mistrust; from this time forward I absolve thee, and do thou teach me to act so that I may throw Palestrina to the ground. I can lock and unlock Heaven, as thou knowest; wherefor the keys are two, which my predecessor held not dear.' Then his weighty arguments pushed me to where silence seemed to me the worst, and I said: 'Father, since thou dost wash me of that sin wherein I now must fall, long promise with short keeping will make thee triumph on the High Seat.' Francis came for me afterwards, when I was dead, but one of the black Cherubim said to him: 'Bear him not away; do me not wrong; he must come down among my drudges because he gave the fraudulent counsel, since which till now I have been at his hair; for he who does not repent cannot be absolved, nor can repentance and will exist together, because of the contradiction which does not allow it.' O me woeful! how I shuddered when he took me, saying to me: 'Perhaps thou didst not think that I was a logician.' He bore me to Minos; and he twisted his tail eight times round his hard back, and, after he had bitten it from great rage, he said: 'This is one of the sinners of the thievish fire:' wherefore here, where thou seest, I am lost, and going thus robed I am afflicted." When he had thus completed his speech the flame, sorrowing, departed, twisting and flapping its sharp horn.

We passed onward, I and my Leader, over the crag, far as to the next arch that covers the ditch in which the fee is paid by those who acquire their load by sundering.

CANTO XXVIII

Eighth Circle: ninth pouch: sowers of discord and schism.—Mahomet and Ali.—Fra Dolcino.—Pier da Medicina.—Curio.—Mosca.—Bertran de Born.

WHO, EVEN WITH words unfettered[1] could ever tell in full, though many times narrating, of the blood and of the wounds that I now saw? Every tongue assuredly would come short, by reason of our speech and our memory which have small capacity to comprise so much.

If all the people were again assembled, that of old upon the storm-tossed land of Apulia lamented for their blood shed by the Trojans,[2] and in the long war that made such vast spoil of the rings, as Livy writes, who does not err; together with those who, by resisting Robert Guiscard, felt the pain of blows, and the others whose bones are still heaped up at Ceperano, where every Apulian was false, and there by Tagliacozzo, where the old Alardo conquered without arms,—and one should show his limb pierced through, and one his lopped off, it would be nothing to equal the hideous mode of the ninth pouch.

Truly a cask by losing mid-board or stave is not so split open, as one I saw who was cleft from the chin to where the wind is broken: his entrails were hanging between his legs, his pluck was visible, and the dismal sack which makes ordure of what is swallowed. While I fix myself all on seeing him, he looked at me, and with his hands opened his breast, saying: "Now see how I rend myself; see how mangled is Mahomet. In front of me goes Ali[3] weeping, cleft in the face from chin to forelock; and all the others whom thou seest here were, when living, sowers of scandal and of schism, and therefore are they so cleft. A devil is here behind that fashions us so cruelly, putting again to the edge of the sword each of this throng, when we have circled the doleful road; because the wounds are closed up before one passes again before him. But who art thou that art musing on the crag, perhaps to delay going to the punishment that has been adjudged on thine own accusations?" "Death has not reached him yet," replied my Master, "nor does guilt lead him to torment him; but, in order to give him full experience, it behoves me, who am dead, to lead him down here through Hell, from circle to circle; and this is true, as that I speak to thee."

More than a hundred there were who, when they

heard him, stopped in the ditch to look at me, forgetting the torment in their wonder.

"Now say then to Fra Dolcino, thou who perhaps wilt shortly see the sun, if he wish not speedily to follow me hither, so to arm himself with provisions that stress of snow may not bring the victory to the Novarese, which to gain otherwise would not be easy." Mahomet said to me this word, after he had lifted one foot to go on, then to depart he stretched it on the ground.

Another who had his throat pierced and his nose cut off close under his brows, and had but one ear only, having stopped to gaze, for wonder, with the others, before the others opened his gullet, which outwardly was all crimson, and said: "O thou whom guilt does not condemn, and whom I saw above in the land of Italy, if exceeding resemblance deceive me not, if ever thou return to see the sweet plain which slopes from Vercelli to Marcabò, remember Pier da Medicina, and make known to the two best men of Fano, to Messer Guido and likewise to Angiolello, that, if our foresight here is not vain, they will be thrown out of their vessel and sunk near La Cattolica, through the treachery of a fell tyrant. Between the islands of Cyprus and Majorca Neptune never saw so great a crime, not of the pirates, nor of the Argolic people. That traitor who sees only with one eye, and holds the city from sight of which one who is here with me would wish he had fasted, will make them come to parley with him; then will deal so that against the wind of Focara they will not need vow or prayer." And I to him: "Show to me and declare, if thou wishest that I carry up news of thee, who is he of the bitter sight?" Then he put his hand on the jaw of one of his companions, and opened the mouth of him, crying: "This is he, and he does not speak; this one, being banished, stifled the doubt in Cæsar, affirming that the man prepared always suffered harm from delay." Oh, how aghast, with his tongue cut off in his throat, seemed to me Curio, who had been so bold to speak!

And one who had both hands lopped off, lifting the stumps through the murky air so that the blood made his face foul, cried out: "Thou shalt bear in mind Mosca, too, who said, alas! 'Thing done has a head,' which was the seed of ill for the Tuscan people." And I added for him: "And death to thine own race." Whereat he, accumulating woe on woe, went away like a person sorrowful and mad.

But I remained to look at the crowd, and saw a thing which, without more proof, I should be afraid only to tell, were it not that conscience reassures me, the good companion which emboldens man under the hauberk of feeling itself pure. I saw truly, and I seem to see it still, a trunk without a head going along, even as the others of the dismal herd were going. And it was holding its cut-off head by the hair, dangling it in hand like a lantern, and that was gazing on us, and saying: "O me!" Of itself it was making a lamp for itself; and they were two in one, and one in two; how it can be He knows who so ordains. When he was right at foot of the bridge, he lifted his arm high with the whole head, in order to bring its words near to us, which were: "Now see the dire punishment, thou that, breathing, goest seeing the dead: see if any other be great as this! And that thou mayst carry news of me, know that I am Bertran de Born,[4] he that gave to the young king the ill encouragements. I made father and son rebels to each other. Ahithophel did not more with Absalom and with David by his wicked goadings. Because I divided persons thus united, I carry my brain, alas! divided from its source which is in this trunk. Thus the retribution is observed in me."

Canto XXIX

Eighth Circle: ninth pouch.—Geri del Bello.—
Tenth pouch: falsifiers of all sorts.—Alchemists.—
Griffolino of Arezzo.—Capocchio.

THE MANY PEOPLE and the divers wounds had so ine-
briated my eyes that they were fain to stay for
weeping; but Virgil said to me: "What art thou still
watching? why does thy gaze still rest down there
among the dismal mutilated shades? Thou hast not done
so at the other pits; consider, if thou thinkest to count
them, that the valley circles two and twenty miles;[1] and
already the moon is beneath our feet; the time is little
now that is conceded to us, and other things are to be
seen than these thou seest." "If thou hadst," replied I
thereupon, "given heed to the reason why I was looking,
perhaps thou wouldst have permitted me yet to stay."

Meanwhile my Leader was going on, and I was going

behind him, now making my reply, and adding: "Within that hollow where I was now holding my eyes so fixedly, I believe that a spirit of my own blood is weeping for the guilt which costs so dear down there." Then said the Master: "Let not thy thought henceforth be broken upon him; attend to other thing, and let him stay there; for I saw him at the foot of the little bridge, pointing thee out, and threatening fiercely with his finger, and I heard him called Geri del Bello. Thou wert then so wholly occupied with him who of old held Hautefort that thou didst not look that way; so he went off." "O my Leader," said I, "that his violent death has not yet been avenged for him by any one who is a partner in the shame made him indignant; wherefore, as I deem, he went on without speaking to me, and thereby he has made me the more pitiful for him."

Thus we spoke as far as the first place on the crag which shows the next valley, if more light were there, quite to the bottom. When we were above the last cloister of Malebolge, so that its lay brothers could appear to our sight, divers lamentations pierced me, which had their arrows barbed with woe; wherefore I covered my ears with my hands.

Such suffering as there would be if, between July and September, the sick from the hospitals of Valdichiana and of Maremma and of Sardinia[2] were all in one ditch together, such was there here; and such stench came forth there-from, as is wont to come from gangrened limbs. We descended upon the last bank of the long crag, ever to the left hand, and then my sight became livelier down toward the bottom, where the ministress of the High Lord—infallible Justice—punishes the falsifiers whom she registers here.

I do not believe it was a greater sorrow to see the whole people in Aegina sick, when the air was so full of harm that the animals, even to the little worm, all fell dead, and afterwards the ancient people, according as the poets hold for sure, were restored from seed of ants, than it was to see the spirits languishing in different heaps through that dark valley. One was lying on the belly, and one on the shoulders of another, and one, on all fours, was shifting himself along the dismal path. Step by step we went without speech, looking at and listening to the sick, who could not lift their persons.

I saw two seated leaning on each other, as pan is leaned against pan to warm, spotted from head to foot with scabs; and never did I see currycomb plied by stable-boy for whom his lord is waiting, or by one who stays awake unwillingly, as each was incessantly plying the bite of his nails upon himself, because of the great rage of his itching which has no other relief. And the nails were dragging down the scab, as a knife does the scales of bream, or of other fish that has them larger still.

"O thou, that art dismailing thyself with thy fingers," began my Leader unto one of them, "and who sometimes makest pincers of them, tell me if any Italian is among those who are here within, so may thy nails suffice thee eternally for this work." "Italians are we whom here thou seest so spoiled, both of us," replied one weeping, "but who art thou that askest of us?" And the Leader said: "I am one that descends with this living man down from ledge to ledge, and I intend to show Hell to him." Then their mutual support was broken; and each turned trembling to me, with others who heard him by rebound. The good Master drew quite

close to me, saying: "Say to them what thou wilt;" and I
began, since he wished it: "So may memory of you in
the first world not steal away from the minds of men,
but may it live under many suns, tell me who ye are,
and of what folk; let not your unseemly and loathsome
punishment fright you from disclosing yourselves unto
me." "I was of Arezzo," replied one of them, "and Al-
bero of Siena had me put in the fire; but that for which
I died does not bring me here. It is true that I said to
him, speaking in jest, that I knew how to raise myself
through the air in flight, and he, who had lively desire
and little wit, wished that I should show him the art,
and only because I did not make him Daedalus, caused
me to be burned by one who had him for son; but to
the last pouch of the ten, Minos, to whom it is not al-
lowed to err, condemned me by reason of the alchemy
that I practiced in the world."

And I said to the Poet: "Now was ever people so vain
as the Sienese? surely not so the French by much."

Whereon the other leprous one, who heard me,
replied to my words: "Excepting Stricca, who knew how
to make moderate spendings; and Niccolò, who first in-
vented the costly use of the clove, in the garden where
such seed takes root; and excepting the brigade in
which Caccia of Asciano squandered his vineyard and
his great wood, and Abbagliato showed his wit. But that
thou mayst know who thus seconds thee against the
Sienese, sharpen thine eye toward me so that my face
may answer well to thee, so wilt thou see that I am the
shade of Capocchio, who falsified the metals by
alchemy; and thou shouldst recollect, if I descry thee
aright, how I was a good ape of nature."[3]

CANTO XXX

AT THE TIME when Juno was wroth because of
Semele against the Theban blood, as she showed
more than once, Athamas became so insane, that seeing
his wife come laden on either hand with her two sons,
he cried out: "Spread we the nets, so that I may take
the lioness and the young lions at the pass," and then he
stretched out his pitiless talons, seizing the one who
was named Learchus, and whirled him and clashed him
on a rock; and she drowned herself with her other bur-
den. And when Fortune turned downward[1] the lofti-
ness of the Trojans which dared all, so that together
with his kingdom the king was undone, Hecuba, sad,
wretched, and captive, after she saw Polyxena dead,

and descried her Polydorus on the sea-strand, she the doleful, frantic, barked like a dog, to such degree had grief distraught her mind.

But neither furies of Thebes nor of Troy were ever seen in any one so cruel, not in goading beasts much less human limbs, as those I saw in two pale and naked shades who were running, biting, in the way that a boar does when he is let out from the sty. One came at Capocchio, and struck his tusks in the nape of his neck, so that dragging him it made his belly scratch along the solid bottom. And the Aretine, who remained trembling, said to me: "That mad sprite is Gianni Schicchi,[2] and he goes rabid dressing others thus." "Oh!" said I to him, "so may the other not fix its teeth on thee, let it not be weariness to thee to tell who it is before it breaks away from here." And he to me: "That is the ancient soul of infamous Myrrha, who became loving of her father beyond rightful love. She came thus to sinning with him by falsifying herself in another's form, even as the other, who goes off there, ventured, in order to gain the lady of the stud, to simulate in his own person Buoso Donati, making a will and giving to the will due form."

And after the two rabid ones, upon whom I had kept my eye, had passed on, I turned it to look at the others of the evil born. I saw one shaped in fashion of a lute, had he only had his groin cut short at the part where man is forked. The heavy dropsy which, with its ill-digested humor, so unmates the members that the face does not correspond with the belly, was making him hold his lips open, as the hectic does, who for thirst turns one toward his chin, and the other upward.

"Oh ye, who are without any punishment, and I know not why, in this dismal world," said he to us, "behold and consider the misery of Master Adam. Living, I had enough of what I wished, and now, alas! I long for a drop of water. The little brooks that from the green hills of the Casentin run down into the Arno, making their channels cool and soft, stand ever before me, and not in vain; for their image dries me up far more than the malady whereby I strip my face of flesh. The rigid justice that scourges me draws occasion from the place where I sinned to set my sighs the more in flight. There is Romena, where I falsified the coin stamped with the Baptist, for which on earth I left my body burnt. But if I could see here the miserable soul of Guido, or of Alessandro, or of their brother, I would not give the sight for Fonte Branda. One of them is here within already, if the raging shades who go around speak true; but what does it avail me who have my limbs bound? If I were only still so light that in a hundred years I could go one inch, I should already have set out along the path, seeking for him among this disfigured folk, although it circles round eleven miles, and has not here less than a half mile across. Because of them I am among such a family; they induced me to strike the florins which had three carats of base-metal."[3] And I to him: "Who are the two poor wretches that are smoking like wet hands in winter, lying close to thy confines on the right?" "Here I found them," he answered, "when I rained down into this trough, and they have not since given a turn, and I do not believe they will give one to all eternity. One is the false woman who accused Joseph, the other is the false Sinon[4] the Greek, from

Troy: because of their sharp fever they throw out such great reek."

And one of them, who took it ill perhaps to be named so darkly, with his fist struck him on his stiff paunch; it sounded as if it were a drum; and Master Adam struck him on the face with his arm which did not seem less hard, saying to him: "Though moving be taken from me because of my limbs which are heavy, I have an arm free for such need." Whereon he replied: "When thou wast going to the fire thou hadst it not thus ready; but so and more thou hadst it when thou wast coining." And he of the dropsy: "Thou sayest true of this, but thou wast not so true a witness there where thou wast questioned of the truth at Troy." "If I said false, thou didst falsify the coin," said Sinon, "and I am here for a single sin, and thou for more than any other demon." "Remember, perjurer, the horse," answered he who had the puffed up paunch, "and be it ill for thee that all the world knows it." "And for thee be ill the thirst wherewith thy tongue cracks," said the Greek, "and the putrid water that makes thy belly thus a hedge before thine eyes." Then the coiner: "Thy mouth gapes thus for its own harm as it is wont, for if I have thirst, and humor stuffs me, thou hast the burning, and the head that pains thee, and to lick the mirror of Narcissus thou wouldst not want many words of invitation."

I was wholly fixed in listening to them, when the Master said to me: "Now only look! for it wants but little that I quarrel with thee." When I heard him speak to me with anger, I turned me toward him with such shame that even yet it circles through my memory. And as is he who dreams of his harm, and, dreaming, desires to dream, so that he longs for that which is, as if it were not, such I became, not being able to speak; for I desired to excuse myself, and all the while I was excusing myself, and never thought that I was doing it. "Less shame washes away a greater fault than thine has been," said the Master; "therefore disburden thyself of all sadness, and make reckoning that I am always at thy side, if again it happen that fortune find thee where people may be in a similar wrangle; for the wish to hear this is a base wish."

Canto XXXI

---

*The Giants around the Eighth Circle.—Nim-
rod.—Ephialtes.—Antaeus sets the Poets down in
the Ninth Circle.*

ONE AND THE same tongue first stung me, so that it
tinged both my cheeks, and then supplied the
medicine to me. Thus do I hear that the lance of
Achilles and of his father was wont to be cause first of a
sad and then of a good gift.

We turned our backs to the wretched valley, up over
the bank that girds it round, crossing without any
speech. Here it was less than night and less than day, so
that my sight went little forward; but I heard a loud
horn sounding, so that it would have made every thun-
der faint, and this directed my eyes, following its course
counter to it, wholly to one place.

After the dolorous rout when Charlemagne lost the

holy gest, Roland sounded not so terribly. Short while I
carried my head turned thitherward, when it seemed to
me that I saw many high towers; whereon I: "Master,
say, what city is this?" And he to me: "Because thou
dost cross through the darkness from too far off, it hap-
pens that then thou dost err in thy imagining. Thou wilt
see well, if thou drawest nigh there, how much the
sense is deceived at a distance; therefore spur thyself
on somewhat more." Then he took me tenderly by the
hand, and said: "Before we go further forward, in order
that the fact may seem less strange to thee, know that
these are not towers, but giants, and they are in the pit
round about the bank, from the navel downward, one
and all of them."

As when the mist is dissipating, the look little by lit-
tle shapes out what the vapor that thickens the air con-
ceals, so, as I pierced the gross and dark air, as we drew
nearer and nearer to the brink, error fled from me and
fear grew upon me. For as above its circular enclosure
Montereggione crowns itself with towers, so with half
their bodies the horrible giants, whom Jove still threat-
ens from heaven when he thunders, betowered the
bank which surrounds the pit.

And already I discerned the face of one of them, his
shoulders, and his breast, and great part of his belly,
and down along his sides both his arms. Nature, surely,
when she left the art of such like living beings, did ex-
ceeding well to take such executioners from Mars: and
though she repent not of elephants and of whales, he
who looks subtly holds her therein more just and more
discreet;[1] for where the faculty of the mind is added to
evil will and to power, the human race can make no de-

fense against it. His face seemed to me long and huge as the pinecone of St. Peter at Rome,[2] and his other bones were in proportion with it; so that the bank, which was an apron from his middle downward, showed of him fully so much above, that three Frieslanders would have made ill vaunt to reach to his hair: for I saw of him thirty great spans down from the place where one buckles his cloak.

"*Rafel mai amech zabi almi*," the fierce mouth, to which sweeter psalms were not befitting, began to cry. And my Leader toward him: "Foolish soul! Keep to thy horn, and with that vent thyself, when anger or other passion touches thee; seek at thy neck, and thou wilt find the cord that holds it tied, O soul confused! and see it lying athwart thy great breast." Then he said to me: "He accuses himself; this is Nimrod, because of whose evil thought one language only is not used in the world. Let us leave him alone, and not speak in vain; for such is every language to him, as his to others which is known to no one."

Then turning to the left, we made a longer journey, and at a crossbow-shot we found the next, far more fierce and larger. Who had been the master to bind him I cannot tell; but he had his right arm shackled behind, and the other in front, by a chain which held him girt from the neck downward, so that upon his uncovered part it was wound as far as the fifth coil. "This proud one wished to make trial of his power against the supreme Jove," said my Leader, "wherefore he has such requital. Ephialtes is his name, and he made his great endeavors when the giants caused fear to the Gods: the arms which he plied he moves nevermore."

And I to him: "If it may be, I would that my eyes might have experience of the measureless Briareus." Whereon he answered: "Hard by here thou shalt see Antaeus, who speaks, and is unfettered, who will set us at the bottom of all sin. He whom thou wishest to see is much farther on, and is bound and fashioned like this one, save that he seems more ferocious in his look."

Never was earthquake so mighty that it shook a tower as violently as Ephialtes was quick to shake himself. Then more than ever did I fear death; and for it there had been no need of more than the fright, if I had not seen his bonds.

We then proceeded further forward, and came to Antaeus, who stood full five ells, besides his head, above the rock. "O thou that, in the fateful valley which made Scipio the heir of glory, when Hannibal with his followers turned his back, didst once bring a thousand lions for booty, and who hadst thou been at the high war of thy brothers, it seems that some still believe that the sons of the Earth would have conquered, set us below (and disdain not to do so) where the cold locks up Cocytus. Make us not go to Tityus, nor to Typhon; this man can give of that which is longed for here; therefore stoop, and twist not thy muzzle. He can yet restore fame to thee in the world; for he is living, and still expects long life, if Grace does not untimely call him to itself." Thus said the Master: and he in haste stretched out those hands, of which Hercules once felt the mighty grip, and took my Leader. Virgil, when he felt himself taken up, said to me: "Come hither, so that I may take thee:" then he did so that he and I were one bundle. As the Carisenda seems to the view, beneath its leaning side, when a cloud is going over it so that the tower hangs counter to it, thus seemed Antaeus to me who was watching to see him stoop; and it was a moment when I could have wished to go by another road. But lightly in the depth that swallows Lucifer with Judas he set us down; nor, thus stooping, did he there make stay, but like the mast of a ship he raised himself.

CANTO XXXII

Ninth Circle: traitors. First ring: Caina.—Counts of Mangona.—Camicion de' Pazzi.—Second ring: Antenora.—Bocca degli Abati.—Buoso da Duera.—Count Ugolino.

IF I HAD rhymes both harsh and raucous, such as would befit the dismal hole on which all the other rocks thrust, I would press out more fully the juice of my conception; but since I have them not, not without fear I bring myself to speak; for to describe the bottom of the whole universe is no enterprise to take up in jest, nor for a tongue that cries mamma and papa. But may those Dames[1] aid my verse, who aided Amphion to enclose Thebes, so that the speech may not be diverse from the fact.

O ye, beyond all others, miscreated rabble, that are in the place whereof to speak is hard, better had ye here been sheep or goats!

When we were down in the dark pit beneath the feet of the giant, far lower, and I was still gazing at the high wall, I heard say to me: "Take heed how thou steppest; go so that thou trample not with thy soles the heads of thy wretched weary brothers." Whereat I turned, and saw before me, and under my feet, a lake which by reason of frost had semblance of glass and not of water.[2]

The Danube in Austria never made in winter so thick a veil for its current, nor the Don yonder under the cold sky, as there was here: for if Tambernich had fallen on it, or Pietrapana, it would not have given a creak even at the edge. And as the frog lies to croak with muzzle out of the water, what time the peasant woman often dreams of gleaning, so, livid up to where shame appears, were the woeful shades within the ice, setting their teeth to the note of the stork.[3] Every one held his face turned downward: from the mouth the cold, and from the eyes the sad heart provides testimony of itself among them.

When I had looked round awhile, I turned to my feet, and saw two so close that they had the hair of their heads mixed together. "Tell me, ye who thus press tight your breasts," said I, "who are ye?" And they bent their necks, and after they had raised their faces to me, their eyes, which before were moist only within, gushed up through the lids, and the frost bound the tears between them, and locked them up again; clamp never girt board to board so strongly: and thereupon they, like two he-goats, butted one another, such anger overcame them.

And one who had lost both his ears by the cold, with his face still downward, said to me: "Why dost thou so mirror thyself on us? If thou wouldst know who are these two, the valley whence the Bisenzio descends belonged to their father Albert, and to them. They issued from one body; and thou mayst search all Caina, and thou wilt not find shade more worthy to be fixed in ice; not he whose breast and shadow were broken by one self-same blow by the hand of Arthur; not Focaccia; not this one who so encumbers me with his head that I see no further, and who was named Sassol Mascheroni; if thou art a Tuscan, thou now knowest well who he was. And that thou mayst not put me to more speech, know that I was Camicion de' Pazzi, and I await Carlino to exculpate me."

Then I saw a thousand faces made currish[4] by the cold: whence a shudder comes to me, and will always come, at frozen pools.

And while we were going toward the centre to which all gravity collects, and I was trembling in the eternal chill, whether it was will, or destiny, or fortune I know not, but, walking among the heads, I struck my foot hard in the face of one. Wailing he railed at me: "Why dost thou kick me? If thou dost not come to increase the vengeance of Mont' Aperti, why dost thou molest me?" And I: "My Master, now wait here for me, so that by means of this one I may free me from a doubt, then thou shalt make as much haste for me as thou wilt." The Leader stopped; and I said to that shade who was still bitterly blaspheming: "Who art thou that thus chidest another?" "Now who art thou, that goest through the Antenora," he answered, "smiting the cheeks of others, so that if thou wert alive, it would be too much?" "I am alive, and it may be dear to thee," was my reply, "if thou demandest fame, that I set thy name among my other notes." And he to me: "For the contrary have I desire; take thyself hence, and give me no more trouble, for ill thou knowest to flatter on this swamp." Then I took him by the hair of the nape, and said: "It shall needs be that thou name thyself, or that not a hair remain upon thee here." Whereon he to me, "Though thou strip me of hair, I will not tell thee who I am, nor show it to thee, though thou fall a thousand times upon my head."

I had already twisted his hair in my hand, and had pulled out more than one tuft, he barking, with his eyes kept close down, when another cried out: "What ails thee, Bocca? Is it not enough for thee to make a noise with thy jaws, but thou must bark too? What devil is at thee?" "Now," said I, "I do not want thee to speak, accursed traitor, for to thy shame will I carry true news of thee." "Begone," he answered, "and tell what thou wilt; but be not silent, if thou go forth from here within, about him who now had his tongue so ready. He is lamenting here the silver of the French: I saw, thou canst say, him of Duera, there where the sinners stand cold. Shouldst thou be asked who else was there, thou hast at thy side him of the Beccheria whose gorge Florence cut. Gianni de' Soldanier I think is farther on with Ganelon, and Tribaldello who opened Faenza when it was sleeping."

We had now departed from him, when I saw two frozen in one hole, so that the head of one was a hood for the other. And as bread is devoured for hunger, so the upper one set his teeth upon the other where the brain joins with the nape. Not otherwise Tydeus gnawed for despite the temples of Menalippus,[5] than this one was doing to the skull and the other parts. "O thou that by so bestial a sign showest hatred against him whom thou art eating, tell me the wherefore," said I, "with this compact, that if thou with reason complainest of him, I, knowing who ye are, and his sin, may yet make thee quits with him in the world above, if that with which I speak be not dried up."

Canto XXXIII

Ninth circle: traitors. Second ring: Antenora.—
Count Ugolino.—Third ring: Ptolomea.—Brother
Alberigo.—Branca d' Oria.

From his savage repast that sinner raised his mouth, wiping it with the hair of the head that he had spoiled behind: then he began: "Thou wishest that I should renew a desperate grief which oppresses my heart already only in thinking, ere I speak of it. But, if my words are to be seed that may bear fruit of infamy for the traitor whom I gnaw, thou shalt see me speak and weep together. I know not who thou art, nor by what mode thou art come down here, but Florentine thou seemest to me truly when I hear thee. Thou hast to know that I was Count Ugolino and this one the Archbishop Ruggieri.[1] Now I will tell thee why I am such a neighbor. That, by the effect of his evil thoughts,

I, trusting to him, was taken and then put to death, there is no need to tell; but what thou canst not have heard, that is, how cruel my death was, thou shalt hear, and shalt know if he has wronged me.

"A narrow slit in the mew, which from me has the title of Hunger, and in which others must yet be shut up, had already shown me through its opening many moons, when I had the bad dream which rent for me the veil of the future.

"This one appeared to me master and lord, chasing the wolf and his whelps upon the mountain because of which the Pisans cannot see Lucca. With lean, eager, and trained hounds, he had put before him at the front Gualandi with Sismondi and with Lanfranchi. After short course, the father and his sons seemed to me weary, and it seemed to me I saw their flanks ripped by the sharp fangs.

"When I awoke before the morrow, I heard my sons, who were with me, wailing in their sleep, and asking for bread. Truly thou art cruel if already thou dost not grieve, at thought of that which my heart was foreboding: and if thou dost not weep, at what art thou wont to weep? They were now awake, and the hour was drawing near at which food used to be brought to us, and because of his dream each one was apprehensive. And I heard the door below of the horrible tower being nailed up; whereat I looked on the faces of my sons without saying a word. I did not weep, I was so turned to stone within. They were weeping; and my poor little Anselm said, 'Thou lookest so, father, what ails thee?' I shed no tear for that; nor did I answer all that day, nor the night after, until the next sun came forth upon the world.

When a little ray made its way into the woeful prison, and I discerned by their four faces my own very aspect, I bit both my hands for woe; and they, thinking I did it through desire of eating, of a sudden raised themselves up, and said: 'Father, it will be far less pain to us if thou eat of us; thou didst clothe us with this wretched flesh, and do thou strip it off.' I quieted me then, not to make them more sad: that day and the next we all stayed dumb. Ah, thou hard earth! why didst thou not open? After we had come to the fourth day, Gaddo threw himself stretched out at my feet, saying: 'My father, why dost thou not help me?' Here he died: and, even as thou seest me, I saw the three fall one by one between the fifth day and the sixth; then I betook me, already blind, to groping over each, and for two days I called them after they were dead: then fasting was more powerful than woe."

When he had said this, with his eyes twisted, he seized again the wretched skull with his teeth, that were strong as a dog's upon the bone.

Ah Pisa! reproach of the people of the fair country where the *sì* doth sound, since thy neighbors are slow to punish thee, let Caprara and Gorgona move and make a hedge for Arno at its mouth, so that it may drown every person in thee: for even if Count Ugolino had repute of having betrayed thee in thy strongholds, thou oughtest not to have set his sons on such a cross. Their young age, thou modern Thebes, made Uguccione and Il Brigata innocent, and the other two that my song names above.

We passed onward to where the ice roughly enswathes another folk, not turned downward, but all reversed.[2] The very weeping allows not weeping there, and the grief, which finds a barrier on the eyes, turns inward to increase the anguish; for the first tears form a block, and like a visor of crystal fill all the cup beneath the eyebrow.

And although, as in a callus, all feeling, because of the cold, had ceased to abide in my face, it now seemed to me I felt some wind, wherefore I: "My Master, who moves this? Is not every vapor quenched here below?" Whereon he to me, "Speedily shalt thou be where thine eye, beholding the cause that rains down the blast, shall make answer to thee of this."

And one of the wretches of the cold crust cried out to us: "O souls so cruel that the last station has been given to you, lift from my eyes the hard veils, so that, before the weeping recongeal, I may vent a little the woe which swells my heart." Wherefore I to him: "If thou wishest that I succor thee, tell me who thou art, and if I relieve thee not, may I have to go to the bottom of the ice." He replied then: "I am friar Alberigo; I am he of the fruits of the bad garden, who here get back a date for a fig."[3] "Oh!" said I to him, "art thou then dead already?" And he to me, "How my body may fare in the world above I have no knowledge. Such vantage hath this Ptolomea that oftentimes the soul falls down here before Atropos has given motion to it.[4] And that thou mayst the more willingly scrape the glassy tears from my face, know that soon as the soul betrays, as I did, its body is taken from it by a demon, who thereafter governs it until its time be all revolved. It falls headlong into such cistern as this, and perhaps the body of the shade that is wintering here behind me still appears above. Thou shouldst know him if thou comest down but now; he is Ser Branca d' Oria, and many years have passed since he was thus shut up." "I believe," said I to him, that thou art deceiving me; for Branca d' Oria is not yet dead, and he eats, and drinks, and sleeps, and puts on clothes." "In the ditch of the Malebranche above," he said, "there where the sticky pitch is boiling, Michel Zanche had not yet arrived, when this one left a devil in his stead in his own body, and in that of one of his next kin, who committed the treachery together with him. But now stretch hither thy hand; open my eyes for me." And I did not open them for him, and to be churlish to him was courtesy.

Ah Genoese! men strange to all morality and full of all corruption, why are ye not scattered from the world? For with the worst spirit of Romagna I found one of you, such that for his deeds he is already in soul bathed in Cocytus, and in body he appears still alive on earth.

CANTO XXXIV

Ninth Circle: traitors. Fourth ring: Judecca.—
Lucifer.—Judas, Brutus and Cassius.—Centre of
the universe.—Passage from Hell.—Ascent to the
surface of the Southern Hemisphere.

"V EXILLA REGIS PRODEUNT INFERNI[1] toward us; there-
fore look forward," said my Master; "see if thou
discern him." As when a thick fog breathes, or when
our hemisphere darkens to night, a mill which the wind
is turning seems from afar, such a structure it seemed
to me that I then saw.

Then, because of the wind, I drew me behind my
Leader; for no other shelter was there. I was now
(and with fear I put it into verse), there where the
shades were wholly covered,[2] and showed through
like a straw in glass. Some are lying down; some are
upright, this one with his head, and that with his

soles uppermost; another, like a bow, bends his face to his feet.

When we had gone so far forward that it pleased my Master to show me the creature which had the fair semblance, he took himself from before me and made me stop, saying: "Lo Dis! and lo the place where it is needful that thou arm thyself with fortitude!" How frozen and faint I then became, ask it not, Reader, for I do not write it, because all speech would be little. I did not die, and did not remain alive: think now for thyself, if thou hast a grain of wit, what I became, deprived of one and the other.

The emperor of the woeful realm issued forth from the ice from the middle of his breast; and I compare better with a giant, than the giants do with his arms. See now how great must be that whole which is conformed to such a part. If he was as fair as he now is foul, and lifted up his brows against his Maker, well should all tribulation proceed from him. Oh how great a marvel it seemed to me, when I saw three faces on his head! one in front, and that was crimson; the others were two, which were adjoined to this above the very middle of each shoulder, and they were joined up to the place of the crest; and the right seemed between white and yellow, the left was such in appearance as those who come from there whence the Nile descends.[3] Beneath each came forth two great wings, of size befitting so great a bird; sails of the sea I never saw such. They had no feathers, but their fashion was of a bat; and he was flapping them so that three winds were proceeding from him, whereby Cocytus was all congealed. With six eyes he was weeping, and over three chins were trickling the tears and bloody drivel. At each mouth he was crushing a sinner with his teeth, in manner of a heckle, so that he thus was making three of them woeful. To the one in front the biting was nothing to the clawing, whereby sometimes his back remained all stripped of the skin.

"That soul up there which has the greatest punishment," said the Master, "is Judas Iscariot, who has his head within, and plies his legs outside. Of the other two who have their heads downwards, he who hangs from the black muzzle is Brutus; see how he writhes and says not a word; and the other is Cassius, who seems so large-limbed.[4] But the night is rising again; and now we must depart, for we have seen the whole."

As was his pleasure, I clasped his neck, and he took advantage of time and place, and when the wings were wide opened he caught hold on the shaggy flanks; down from shag to shag he then descended between the matted hair and the frozen crusts. When we were where the thigh turns just on the thick of the haunch, my Leader, with effort and stress of breath, turned his head to where he had had his shanks, and grappled to the hair like one who mounts, so that I believed we were returning again to hell.

"Cling fast hold," said the Master, panting like one weary, "for by such stairs must we depart from so great evil." Then he came forth through the cleft of a rock, and placed me upon its edge to sit; then stretched toward me his cautious step.

I raised my eyes, and thought to see Lucifer as I had left him, and I saw him holding his legs upward; and if I then became perplexed, let the dull folk suppose it, who see not what that point is which I had passed.[5]

"Rise up on foot," said the Master; "the way is long and the road is difficult, and already the sun returns to mid-tierce."

It was no hallway of a palace where we were, but a natural dungeon which had a bad floor, and lack of light. "Before I tear myself from the Abyss," said I when I had risen up, "my Master, talk a little with me to draw me out of error. Where is the ice? and this one, how is he fixed thus upside down? and how in such short while has the sun made transit from evening to morning?" And he to me: "Thou imaginest that thou still art on the other side of the centre, where I laid hold on the hair of the wicked Worm that pierces the world. On that side thou wast so long as I descended; when I turned, thou didst pass the point to which from every part all weighty things are drawn; and thou art now arrived beneath the hemisphere which is opposite to that which the great dry land covers, and beneath whose zenith the Man was slain who was born and lived without sin: thou hast thy feet upon a little circle which forms the other face of the Judecca. Here it is morning when it is evening there; and this one who made a ladder for us with his hair is still fixed even as he was before. On this side he fell down from heaven, and the earth, which before was spread out on this side, through fear of him made of the sea a veil, and came to our hemisphere; and perhaps to fly from him that land which appears on this side left here this vacant space and ran back upward."

A place is there below, stretching as far from Beelzebub as his tomb extends, which is not known by sight, but by the sound of a rivulet which descends here along the hollow of a rock that it has gnawed with its winding and gently sloping course. My Leader and I entered by that hidden road, to return into the bright world; and without care to have any repose, we mounted up, he first and I second, so far that through a round opening I saw some of the beautiful things which Heaven bears, and thence we issued forth again to see the stars.

Notes

Canto I

1. **"Midway upon the journey of our life"**: The poem's action begins the night before Good Friday, 1300, in the middle years of Dante's life.

2. **she-leopard**: To the medieval Christian mind, leopards represented the temptations of the flesh, because they are very beautiful but extremely dangerous.

3. **lion**: The lion represents pride, and the she-wolf that appears immediately thereafter represents avarice.

4. **Virgil**: Virgil (70–19 B.C.) is the classical Roman poet, author of the *Aeneid*, the *Eclogues*, and the *Georgics*. He was of towering importance for medieval Christian culture.

5. **there shall be a soul**: The soul in question is Beatrice's. Beatrice is Dante's muse and divine mentor, who throughout *The Divine Comedy* guides him and draws him upward toward Heaven.

6. **gate of St. Peter:** The gate of Saint Peter is the gate of Purgatory, a place where those who die without being fully purged of their sins must wait until they are pure enough to enter Heaven.

Canto II

1. **Muses:** The Muses of classical mythology are the divine daughters of Memory, and they grant the poet power and authorization for his song.
2. **Chosen Vessel:** The chosen vessel is Saint Paul.
3. **"I was among those who are suspended":** The souls of virtuous pagans and of unbaptized children had, before Christ's ascension, no access to saving grace. They were in the place the Church fathers called Limbo, awaiting the triumph of the Lord.
4. **gentle Lady:** The Virgin Mary. She is the source of all mercy and is thus never mentioned in Hell, where mercy is unknown.
5. **Lucia:** A symbol of enlightening grace, a lady of illumination, as her name suggests.
6. **Rachel:** Rachel was associated by the Church with the contemplative life and thus was a natural partner to Beatrice.

Canto III

1. **him who made . . . the great refusal:** The reference is to Pope Celestine V, who abdicated the Papacy in 1294, five months after assuming the position. He was followed by the infamous Pope Boniface VIII, who abused his power in many ways,

including getting Celestine to resign in the first place and then imprisoning him for the rest of his aged life.

2. **Charon:** The mythological ferryman across the River Styx; here the pilot of redeemed souls to Purgatory.

Canto IV

1. **first circle:** Limbo, where Dante imagined unbaptized adults and virtuous pagans went after death.

2. **human spirits were not saved:** Adam and his descendants were considered to be uniformly tainted with original sin, from which Jesus rescued them by his descent into Hell.

3. **noble castle:** The castle symbolizes the home of philosophy, the highest understanding possible to man without divine revelation.

4. **seven gates:** The gates stand for the seven liberal arts, paths to the knowledge of the universe.

5. **Master of those who know:** The reference is to the philosopher Aristotle.

Canto V

1. **Minos:** King of Crete and judge in the underworld.

2. **she who, for love, slew herself:** Dido, Queen of Carthage, who according to Virgil's *Aeneid* killed herself when Aeneas deserted her.

3. **two that go together:** Francesca da Rimini and Paolo Malatesta, her brother-in-law. Francesca's husband discovered them together and killed them both.

Canto VI

1. **"Return to thy science":** Go back to your Aristotle, from whom you will learn that after the Last Judgment the suffering of the damned will increase.
2. **Pluto:** Here Dante blends Plutus, the classical god of wealth, with Hades, the classical god of the underworld.

Canto VII

1. **Wolf:** The wolf is a symbol of avarice.
2. **hymn they gurgle:** The wrathful can only gurgle, because submerged in the River Styx.

Canto VIII

1. **Phlegyas:** A Greek king whose daughter was raped by Apollo. Enraged, Phlegyas burned down Apollo's temple, and here, appropriately, he guards the wrathful.
2. **Dis:** Dis, a Roman name for the ruler of the underworld, is used here to mean the region of the underworld.
3. **those rained down from heaven:** The fallen angels, who have become devils and attempt to obstruct the divine will that is leading Dante on his journey through Hell.

Canto IX

1. **repressed . . . his own new color:** Virgil represses his own misgivings, in view of his ward's pallor.

2. **Erichtho:** a Greek sorceress of legend, who called up the spirit of a dead soldier, that he might predict the future.

3. **three infernal Furies:** The Furies, who in classical myth punish those who have offended the gods, here represent self-torturing passions of understanding, which have fallen prey to perverse self-will.

4. **Gorgon:** The Gorgons of myth are monsters so frightening that a mere glimpse of one would turn a mortal to stone.

Canto X

1. **Jehoshaphat:** The Valley of Jehoshaphat was thought to be the scene of the Last Judgment, where the bodies of the dead would be reunited with their souls.

2. **Farinata:** Farinata, for many years the head of the Ghibelline party in Florence, twice drove the Guelfs from power, but each time the Guelfs returned.

3. **Lady who rules here:** The reference is to Proserpine, the mythical queen of the underworld, who is also identified with the moon and its mystical powers.

Canto XI

1. **wickedness:** Wickedness implies intentional evil-doing and is distinct from sins arising from lack of self-control.

2. **Cahors:** A city in southern France known in the Middle Ages for usury.

3. **bond of love which nature makes:** That is, the common bond joining fellow humans.

4. **ruddy city:** The city of Dis.

5. **usury offends the Divine Goodness:** Dante wants to be sure he understands the special viciousness of usury.

6. **note thy Physics:** Reference to Aristotle's *Physics*, a central text for the Middle Ages. Art follows nature, as a learner follows his master. Nature is organic and productive, usury is parasitical.

7. **Genesis at its beginnings:** "By the sweat of your brow you will earn your food" (Genesis 3:19).

8. **upon the other thing he sets his hope:** The usurer sets his hope on gain won not from the bounty of nature but from guile, which sidesteps the course of nature.

Canto XII

1. **infamy of Crete:** The Minotaur, a monster with a man's body and a bull's head, offspring of the queen of Crete's bestial mating with a magical bull.

2. **Duke of Athens:** Theseus, who, with the help of Ariadne, daughter of the king and queen of Crete, killed the Minotaur in its labyrinth.

3. **heart that is still honored on the Thames:** In 1271 Prince Henry, Earl of Cornwall, was stabbed to death at mass in Viterbo, Italy. The killer is the "solitary shade" we see here, Guy de Montfort, who was avenging the death of his father. The heart of Prince Henry, it was said, was placed in a golden cup and displayed on a column on London Bridge.

4. **Rinier of Corneto and . . . Rinier Pazzo:** The two Riniers mentioned here were armed robbers who attacked travelers between Rome and Florence.

Canto XIII

1. **things that would take credence from my speech:** Things that, if told, would make my speech seem incredible.
2. **trunk:** The speaker is Pier delle Vigne, chancellor and private secretary to Emperor Frederick II.
3. **harlot . . . vice of courts:** Envy.
4. **Toppo:** Site of a Sienese defeat in which Lano was killed.
5. **Attila:** Not Attila the Hun but Totila, who besieged Florence in 542, and who was frequently confused with Attila in the Middle Ages.

Canto XIV

1. **sand . . . trodden by the feet of Cato:** In a march of the Roman army that he led across the desert of Libya in 47 B.C.
2. **Some folk were lying supine . . . some were seated . . . others were going about:** The three groups of sinners are guilty of violence to God (the supine), violence to Nature (the crouched), and violence to art (those in constant motion).
3. **Bulicame:** A spring near Viterbo, the use of which was reserved for prostitutes.
4. **Damietta:** Eastern mouth of the Nile, hence the East, the origin of mankind.

5. **His head is formed . . . more than the other:** The image is taken from the Dream of Nebuchadnezzar, Daniel 2:31–33. The progression of materials from gold to clay represents the debasement of civilization from its height under the Roman empire.

Canto XV

1. **please him:** Dante never speaks Virgil's name aloud in Hell.
2. **such earnest:** Such warnings of what is to come.
3. **green cloth:** Prize for winning the annual races at Verona.

Canto XVI

1. **this soft place:** Soft because it is sand.
2. **sudden gains:** The population and wealth of Florence increased dramatically in the late thirteenth century.
3.. **leopard of the painted skin:** The leopard, symbolic of sensual excess, that had turned Dante back into the dark wood in Canto I. The wearing of a cord was a well-known ascetic practice.

Canto XVII

1. **wild beast . . . that infects all the world:** Dante makes Geryon into a symbol of all the fraud in the world.
2. **certain device:** The blazon of their arms, normally borne on the family shield, is here borne on the humble purse the sinner carries.

3. **descent is by such stairs:** Monstrous denizens of Hell, not stairs, would now be Dante's means of descent.

Canto XVIII

1. **Malebolge:** Literally, evil pouches, the rings of concentric circles that make up the eighth circle of the fraudulent.
2. **year of the Jubilee:** In the year 1299–1300 Pope Boniface VIII invited hordes of penitent pilgrims to visit the city of Rome. So huge were the crowds that barriers were built on either side of the Sant'Angelo Bridge, so that people going to and from Saint Peter's could move in separate streams.
3. **Ghisola:** The sister of the speaker; he procured her for the marquis in order to gain favor with him.
4. **where it opens:** Reference to the bridge Dante and Virgil are crossing.

Canto XIX

1. **Simon Magus:** See Acts 8:9–24. The magician who offered money to the apostles in an attempt to buy their miraculous powers.
2. **assassin:** Such evildoers were occasionally punished by being placed head downward in a hole and buried alive.
3. **he cried out:** Nicholas III, Pope from 1277 to 1280. He awaits the arrival of Pope Boniface VIII.
4. **beautiful Lady:** The Church.
5. **She-Bear:** The Orsini family. (*Orsa* = she bear.)

6. **"Follow thou me"**: John 21:19.
7. **Constantine . . . but that dowry**: The "dowry"
   refers to the Donation of Constantine, a papally
   forged document dating from 750 that asserted the
   first Christian emperor had granted all temporal
   power in the West to the Papacy. The forgery was
   not unmasked until the fifteenth century.

Canto XX

1. **pity lives when it is quite dead**: Compassion is only
   for the living and souls in Purgatory. The dead in Hell
   are unchangeable. It is impious to wish them otherwise.
2. **Tiresias**: The Theban prophet of classical Greek
   myth. He was a hermaphrodite, accidentally blinded
   by the goddess Juno, who made him a prophet in
   compensation.
3. **Manto**: The daughter of Tiresias, also a prophetess.
4. **city of Bacchus**: Thebes.
5. **Eurypylus . . . my lofty tragedy**: In the *Aeneid*
   Virgil wrote of the Greek soothsayer Eurypylus,
   whose prophecies were instrumental in launching
   the Greek fleet into the Trojan War.
6. **Cain with his thorns**: The Man in the Moon. Ital-
   ian legend sees Cain there, with a bundle of thorny
   branches on his back.

Canto XXI

1. **Malebranche**: "Evil-claws."
2. **barrator**: A person who sells or buys public office
   or justice.

3. **Malacoda:** "Evil-tail."
4. **since the way was broken here:** Broken by the earthquake that marked the death of Jesus, thought to have been thirty-three or thirty-four years old at his crucifixion.
5. **Scarmiglione . . . Graffiacane:** The names of these demons are comically obscene: *Scarmiglione* means "disheveled." *Graffiacane* means "scratch dog."

Canto XXII

1. **King Thibault:** Brother-in-law of Saint Louis. He accompanied him on his last Crusade, and died on the way home.

Canto XXIII

1. **leaded glass:** A mirror.
2. **within all lead . . . that those Frederick:** Emperor Frederick II is said to have put leaden cloaks on criminals and then burnt them to death. Those cloaks were light as straw compared to the cloaks of Dante's "painted people."
3. **with eye askance:** Their cloaks were so heavy they could not raise their heads for a full glance.
4. **scales to creak:** The sinners are like overloaded scales that creak under the weight of their cloaks.
5. **That transfixed one . . . weighs:** Caiaphas, who proposed Jesus as scapegoat (John 11:50), now must feel on himself the weight of the sinners who tread across him.
6. **Virgil marvel:** Virgil doesn't know the Gospel and so can't comprehend what he is seeing.

Canto XXIV

1. **part of the young year . . . Aquarius:** Approximately January 20 to February 20.
2. **thus:** With great effort.
3. **chelydri, jaculi . . . phareae . . . cenchri . . . amphisboena:** Names of Libyan snakes, derived from Lucan's first-century description of the plague in Libya.
4. **heliotrope:** A stone thought to make its bearer invisible; ideal for thieves.
5. **mule:** Mule = bastard.

Canto XXV

1. **hands with both the figs:** Gesture of contempt made by thrusting out the fist, the thumb of which has been stuck out between the fore- and middle finger; similar in spirit to the gesture we call "the bird" or "the finger" but representing female rather than male genitals.
2. **Maremma:** The region of Tuscany that borders the sea; considered an unhealthful, swampy area.
3. **whereat our nourishment is first taken:** The navel.
4. **Sabellus . . . Nasidius:** Stung by snakes, Sabellus melted away, and Nasidius swelled until he burst his armor.
5. **drew his feet together:** Making a tail.
6. **wretch . . . stretched forth:** His penis has morphed into two hind feet.

Canto XXVI

1. **he who was avenged:** Elisha, 2 Kings 2:9–24.
2. **fire . . . so divided . . . put with his brother:**
   Eteocles and Polynices, sons of Oedipus and Jocasta,
   slew one another at the battle of Thebes. Their rival-
   rous hatred was so great that their funeral pyre di-
   vided into two flames. Below, Ulysses and Diomede
   are punished for advocating the use of the Wooden
   Horse.
3. **ambush of the horse . . . Palladium:** The
   Wooden Horse concealed the Greek warriors who
   caused the downfall of Troy. The Palladium was the
   image of the goddess Athena, and it had secured the
   safety of Troy; it was stolen by Eteocles and Poly-
   nices.
4. **deep, open sea . . . one shore and the other:**
   The Mediterranean.
5. **bounds . . . out beyond:** Those bounds, known as
   the Pillars of Hercules, were once considered the
   world's limits. Emperor Charles V took them for his
   emblem, with the motto *Più oltre non,* "Go no far-
   ther."

Canto XXVII

1. **besought Sylvester:** Guido reveals here and in the
   following lines the fraudulent counsel for which he
   was damned: He advised Pope Boniface VIII to
   make false pledges of protection to the city of
   Palestrina, in order to disarm and betray the city.

Canto XXVIII

1. **words unfettered:** Free of the "shackles" of formal verse.
2. **Trojans:** The Romans.
3. **Ali:** Son-in-law of Mohammed. Ali's fissure may represent the split between Sunni and Shiite Islam, a schism within the religion.
4. **Bertran de Born:** Eminent troubadour poet, responsible for turning young Prince Henry of England against his father, Henry II.

Canto XXIX

1. **two and twenty miles:** This circumference is Dante's first attempt to give a precise measurement of a region of Hell.
2. **Valdichiana . . . Maremma . . . Sardinia:** Three marshy areas known to be rife with malaria.
3. **ape of nature:** Imitator of nature. The speech suggests that Capocchio had known Dante in the upper world.

Canto XXX

1. **Fortune turned downward:** The Wheel of Fortune, which is always revolving.
2. **Gianni Schicchi:** Elder contemporary of Dante, and famed impersonator, as the following story explains. Impersonation was seen as alienation or madness.

3. **florins . . . base-metal:** Florins that were three carats short of the twenty-four carats of gold required by the law.
4. **false Sinon:** Sinon, a wily Greek who induced the Trojans to let the fatal Wooden Horse into their city.

Canto XXXI

1. **elephants . . . whales . . . discreet:** Elephants and whales lack reason, thus are not as dangerous to mankind as were once these giants.
2. **pine-cone of St. Peter at Rome:** A massive gilt-bronze cone which, in Dante's time, stood in the entranceway of Saint Peter's and now stands at the entrance to a Vatican museum.

Canto XXXII

1. **those Dames:** The Muses. They gave such power to the lyre of Amphion, that at its sound the rocks moved themselves from Mount Cithaeron to build the walls of the city of Thebes.
2. **reason of frost . . . water:** The ice in which the traitors are frozen fits with the icy-cold nature of their hearts. The lake of ice is built around four concentric rings, the inmost and worst of which is Judecca, where traitors are frozen fast to those who helped them.
3. **note of the stork:** The stork clatters its bill, as cold humans chatter their teeth.
4. **currish:** Grinning like dogs.
5. **Tydeus . . . Menalippus:** Tydeus was fatally

wounded by Menalippus while besieging Thebes, but as he died he killed Menalippus and began to gnaw on his enemy's severed head.

Canto XXXIII

1. **Count Ugolino . . . Archbishop Ruggieri:** Ugolino was a leading Guelf citizen of Pisa. Archbishop Ruggiero, a Ghibelline leader, pretended to join forces with him but instead shut him up in the tower where Ugolino met his terrible end.
2. **reversed:** Their faces were turned upward, so that their tears froze in their eyes.
3. **get back a date for a fig:** Alberigo murdered his brother and several relatives at a banquet. The signal for the assassins was "Bring in the fruit." In Hell he is overpaid for his sin: Figs were the cheapest Tuscan fruit, but dates had to be imported, and so cost more.
4. **Atropos has given motion to it:** That is, before this particular Fate had cut the thread of the soul's life on earth.

Canto XXXIV

1. ***Vexilla . . . inferni:*** "The banners of the king of Hell advance."
2. **there where the shades were wholly covered:** In the innermost ice ring of the ninth circle.
3. **three faces . . . Nile descends:** The three faces are diabolical counterparts of the three persons of the Godhead: Impotence, Ignorance, and Hate, contrasting with Power, Wisdom, and Love.

4. **Judas . . . Brutus . . . Cassius:** Judas, Brutus, and Cassius are the worst of the traitors who turned against their benefactors: Judas against Christ and the Church; Brutus and Cassius against Caesar and the Roman Empire. For Dante, Church and empire were coequal benefactors of mankind.

5. **what that point is which I had passed:** The center of the universe, past which Hell instantly appears upside down. Now Dante begins to climb upward again, toward the Mountain of Purgatory.

INTERPRETIVE NOTES

Dante's *Inferno* is the story of a dream vision or theological vision. It is for us today the most comprehensible of the three wonderful segments that compose *The Divine Comedy*—a name given in the sixteenth century to Dante's three-part poetic epic, and carrying that period's sense of "comedy" as an action that ends happily. *The Divine Comedy* includes the *Inferno*, the *Purgatorio*, and the *Paradiso*. It takes us across these three regions in the company of Dante—the character as distinguished from the author—through whose psyche we take a phantasmagorical journey. The *Inferno* is the most widely read of the three segments, and it is certainly engaging on its own, but its full meaning can be appreciated only within the context of the entire *Divine Comedy*.

On the first leg of his journey, Dante passes through Hell, or Inferno. As the story opens, the bewildered Dante, finding himself lost in a dark wood, is beset immediately by unfriendly beasts. To his great relief he is rescued by the ancient Roman poet he and his contemporaries most admire: Virgil, author of the *Aeneid*. Dante's heart swells, for Virgil represents to him the highest poetic wisdom. Dante could not possibly have found a better guide.

The text explains that Virgil, though an unbaptized pagan, is qualified to lead Dante through the Christian Hell, because reason alone (which Virgil has) is sufficient for this mission. At every step, Virgil will counsel the tremulous and intent Dante about the best and safest path to choose. (Virgil's services will no longer be useful in Purgatory or Paradise, for to enter those realms baptism and awareness of Revelation are the necessary prerequisites. It seems that in those higher realms we today feel ourselves less at home; perhaps we, like Virgil, are closer to understanding Hell than we are to understanding Purgatory or Paradise; perhaps many of us are less comfortable with the theology of the higher regions.)

Dante's journey with Virgil is a descent, precipitous at times, toward the center of the earth. It is a craggy and fiery environment that worsens steadily as they descend. Ledge by ledge, often by way of dangerous declivities such as those left by the earthquake believed to have accompanied Christ's crucifixion in 34 A.D., the two travelers make their way through distinctive landscapes in which they meet sinners with identities drawn from ancient and contemporary cultures. The defining sin of each fallen soul—for these are souls, not living bodies like that of Dante the pilgrim—is illustrated in one way or another by the condition in which that person is found. The lustful are

blown by hot winds, the violent against nature are del-
uged by a fiery rain, the embezzlers are submerged in
a river of boiling pitch. The travelers' descent through
the *Inferno* increases in steepness with the severity of
the sinners' conditions and ultimately reaches the low-
est level of human evil, that of the betrayers of God
and country.

Characters

If the *Inferno* can be said to have major and minor
characters, the major ones are of course Dante and Vir-
gil, and the minor are figures from that huge gallery of
sinners we meet on the way down. However, the usual
distinction among kinds of characters in a work of liter-
ature does not apply here. Dante and Virgil are tourists
of the unholy realms. They are figments of Dante's
imagination, except in the important sense that Dante
the author has already completed the journey and
knows from beginning to end the structure he is dis-
playing, while Dante the character is an existential pil-
grim, experiencing the unfolding of reality step by step.
The gallery of minor figures are completely unforeseen
by Dante the pilgrim, who encounters each of them in
shocked surprise, especially those who were previously
known to him in life.

Certain of the characters we meet along sin's way
have become part of world literature in themselves, as
though they were paintings held on permanent display.
Who are some of these classics, and what do they say
to Dante? Let's take Paolo and Francesca (Canto 5),

Brunetto Latini (Canto 15), Mohammed (Canto 28), and Ugolino (Canto 33) as examples:

Paolo and Francesca. Dante and Virgil come upon these two lovers in the sandy, windblown desert proper to those whose sin was reckless passion, a passion that is blown this way and that. While Francesca recalls her fatal moment of adultery, Dante listens with conflicted feelings: God's punishing judgment is not to be second-guessed, but still the power of the passions is gripping and the sad fate touching.

Brunetto Latini. Dante's master in letters and life, a major figure in Florence during Dante's youth, Brunetto comes up to Dante in Hell and walks beside him, at a lower level, as was obligatory for the sinner. The discrepancy in height—Latini's head at the level of Dante's hem—underlines the humiliation of the sinner and provokes great embarrassment in the pilgrim Dante, who had revered him. One sin, homosexuality, divides the two men, and though Brunetto had been otherwise faultless, it has destroyed him and relegated him to this painful place.

Mohammed. Mohammed is met in the circle of schismatics, those who in their lifetime sowed discord. It was widely thought in Dante's Christian world that Mohammed was originally a Nestorian Christian, in line for a cardinalate, when he decided to establish his own religion. There is nothing touching in this canto, which is devoted to such as have been cleft from chin to rectum and drag their innards behind them. The obscene and the grotesque meet in this text as they do in the gargoyles that are the rainspouts of the Gothic cathedrals.

Ugolino. Ugolino's is the most touching story evoked from the sinners in Hell. The charge that has bound the distinguished count in Hell is treachery, which he committed in order to make certain political and military deals that we have difficulty interpreting today. As Ugolino recounts the punishment inflicted on him by his persecutors and opponents, we tremble with Dante at the depths of his suffering: Ugolino and his children were locked in a tower, and the key was thrown into the Arno River. The desperate father, after seeing his children starve to death, was reduced to cannibalism. Time or repentance will not remove such a sin.

Themes

Literature as Conveyor of Immortality. Dante clearly hopes that his magnificent epic work will make him immortal, much as Virgil's work made him immortal. While he is in awe of Virgil, Dante is not shy about bragging that his own literary expertise outshines that of the famous Roman poet Ovid. He takes several opportunities throughout the text to tout his own skill and importance.

Throughout the *Inferno*, it seems the sinners, too, realize that through Dante's future writings their lives might be remembered. They frequently ask their visitor, to record their names and deeds when he returns to the world. Dante sees storytelling of this sort as a powerful and meaningful act, and his role as storyteller is one of awesome responsibility. He refuses, for example, to include in his poem the names of some of the more scurrilous inhabitants of the Eighth Circle who ask him to tell their stories. Yet his declared intention to tell the stories of others runs counter, somewhat, to the main purpose of *The Divine Comedy*—to extoll the perfect justice of God, who has condemned these sinners to eternal punishment in Hell. Through Dante they have been permitted some comfort—they will be remembered again in the world and will perhaps even attract sympathy.

God's Perfection. The elaborate conception of *The Divine Comedy*—a three-part work constructed in terza rima—is meant to reflect the perfection of the Holy Trinity. We don't see this as much in the *Inferno*, but readers must remember that the end—both the final outcome and the whole purpose of the composition—of *The Divine Comedy* is Paradise. In the *Inferno*, however, Dante does remind us that God's justice is absolute and that even Hell was created as part of God's loving, perfect vision. The famous inscription over the gates of Hell that appears in Canto 3 reads: "Justice moved my lofty maker: the divine Power, the supreme Wisdom and the primal Love made me. Before me were no things created, save eternal, and I eternal last. Leave every hope, ye who enter!"

Sin, even to a minor degree, is defined as a contradiction of God's will. Modern readers often question the ranking of the sins in the *Inferno*, and in reality Dante's contemporaries—and even Dante—may have, too. But Dante's work does not question the accepted

Christian doctrine on sin, nor does it offer excuse or explanation for the existence of sin. However, by having some of his characters tell stories of their lives, the *Inferno* allows us the chance to like them and to mourn their fate.

Political Corruption and the Separation of Church and State. Without question, Dante's life was defined by the political forces that tore apart fourteenth-century Florence. As already noted, warring factions—the Guelfs and Ghibellines—struggled for control of Florence from within, while the pope struggled for control from without. There were even factions within factions, as was the case with the Black Guelfs and the White Guelfs. By the time he was writing the *Inferno*, Dante was in bitter exile from his beloved Florence because of the brutal political wranglings of both secular and religious figures. It seems natural that Dante reserved especially unpleasant parts of Hell for those he judged guilty of political misdeeds, usually his own political enemies. The worst sinners of all, for Dante, were traitors—betrayers of God or of country. To Dante, the overlapping of Church and secular powers caused such betrayal, and he condemned power-greedy clerics who sought political positions and money.

CRITICAL EXCERPTS

Biography and Historical/Political Contexts

Curtius, Ernst Robert. "Dante." In *European Literature and the Latin Middle Ages*. Princeton, N.J.: Princeton University Press, 1953.

Curtius is one of the most learned scholars of Latin medieval literature, and therefore one of the best at setting Dante in his cultural context.

> The awakening of Virgil by Dante is an act of flame which leaps from one great soul to another. The tradition of the European spirit knows no situation of such affecting loftiness, tenderness, fruitfulness. It is the meeting of the two greatest Latins.

Mazzeo, Joseph Anthony. *Medieval Cultural Tradition in Dante's Comedy*. Ithaca, N.Y.: Cornell University Press, 1960.

A cultural-historical study of the medieval worldview of the cosmos as a structure of harmonic unity.

A St. Augustine may see all mortal sin as finally, in the eyes of God, equally monstrous, but the very point of having a system of punishments in the *Inferno* is that we are thereby called upon to consider moral evil as something graded and hence understandable as a complex interweaving of worth and negation.

Bergin, Thomas. *An Approach to Dante*. London: The Bodley Head, 1965.
An excellent introductory volume on Dante's life, times, and work, with valuable material on the meaning of Dante for later centuries.

Dante's great work is concerned with matters not of this world; his subject is the afterlife, his pilgrimage takes him into realms which cannot be changed on physical maps, and his interests are in things eternal and not temporal. Yet for all that, he is very much of his century. His thought and his outlook were determined by the events and the theories of his day, and his own temperament made him more than a merely passive receiver of impressions.

Quinones, Ricardo. *Dante Alighieri*. Boston: Twayne Publishers, 1979.
A handy survey of Dante's life and works.

Is Dante only an overreacher, a Phaeton, an Icarus, who is fatally deluded into thinking that outside of his old commune he can find real peace and understanding and that by going beyond the practices of his own time he can write a poem worthy of a place in the line of the great masterpieces of antiquity? He is not Aeneas; he is not Paul.

Ferrante, Joan. *The Political Vision of the Divine Comedy*. Princeton, N.J.: Princeton University Press, 1984.
A close reading of Dante's social beliefs. Ferrante argues that Dante believes social and political morality must precede individual cleanness of soul.

Popes had made extravagant claims and practiced continual intrigues. They were perceived by their enemies as greedy, petty men, leading the Church in the wrong direction and giving a bad example to the Christians they were supposed to guide, and that is how Dante portrays them in the *Comedy*, where the corruption is condemned from the beginning of Hell to the summit of Paradise.

Boyde, Patrick. *Perception and Passion in Dante's Comedy*. New York: Cambridge University Press, 1993.
A technical but thoroughly readable study of Dante's medieval, Aristotle-based theory of how we perceive, see, and feel.

The first line of the *Comedy* tells us that the events to be narrated took place when the narrator was "in the middle of the journey of our life." The words are usually interpreted (with a certain amount of circularity in the reasoning) to yield the very precise sense that it was 1300, when Dante was in his thirty-fifth year. But it is equally possible, and highly desirable, to understand the phrase less narrowly as meaning "in our middle age," that is, in the second of the three ages of man, which, in Dante's view, extends from the twenty-fifth to the forty-fifth year of a normal human life span.

Botterill, Steven. *Dante and the Mystical Tradition: Bernard of Clairvaux in the Commedia*. Cambridge, England: Cambridge University Press, 1994.

A study of Dante's relation to Bernard, the deepest mystic of the twelfth century. Enlightening for an understanding of the entire *Commedia*.

Briefly, my argument is that the *Commedia* is a Heraclitean River, into which no reader can ever step twice and find it unaltered. Less poetically, I would contend that there is a crucial difference between a first reading of the poem and any or all subsequent reading(s); and, equally, that no matter how many times a reader opens a copy of *Inferno* at those mysteriously thrilling words "Nel mezzo del cammin di nostra vita / mi ritrovai in una selva oscura, / ché la diritta via era smarrita" (*Inf.*, 1,1–3), he or she is never setting out again on the same journey, never beginning to read again the same poem. Reading and rereading the *Commedia* are very different propositions.

Critical Interpretations

1930s through 1950s

Grandgent, C. H., editor. Introduction. In *La Divina Commedia di Dante Alighieri*. Boston: D.C. Heath, 1933.

This essay by the great dean of American Dante studies precedes the classical annotated text of the *Commedia*.

When we ask ourselves why we are so strangely stirred by the words of a man of whom we know so little, one so remote in date and in thoughts, we find that it is because, on the one hand, he knew how to present universal emotions, stripping his experiences of all that is peculiar to time or place; and, secondly, because he felt more intensely than other men; his joy, his anguish, his love, his hate, his hope, his faith, were so keen that they come quivering down through the ages and set our hearts in responsive vibration.

Auerbach, Erich. "Farinata and Cavalcante." In *Mimesis: The Representation of Reality in Western Literature*. Princeton, N.J.: Princeton University Press, 1953.
A rich collection of essays on literary style and its capacities for realism in Western literature from Homer to the present.

The existence of the two tomb-dwellers and the scene of it are certainly final and eternal, but they are not devoid of history. This Hell has been visited by Aeneas and Paul and even by Christ; now Dante and Virgil are traveling through it; it has landscapes, and its landscapes are peopled by infernal spirits; occurrences, events, and even transformations go on before our very eyes. In their phantom bodies the souls of the damned, in their eternal abodes, have phenomenal appearance, freedom to speak and gesture and even to move about within limits, and thus, within their changelessness, a limited freedom of change.

1960s and 1970s

Clements, Robert, editor. *American Critical Essays on the Divine Comedy*. New York: New York University Press, 1967.

A wonderful collection of essays by leading Dante scholars on topics ranging from prosody to theology.

He was intense in his imaginative thought, which ranged relentlessly from his own immediate and central soul to the final timelessness and spacelessness of the Empyrean. He was intense in his emotions, whether of hope or of fear, whether of love or hate. He was intent on mastering all the lore that entered the library of his mind, and in transmuting it into the processes of his own living. He was intense in the effort to achieve loyal poetic utterance: in the *Paradiso* he speaks of the *Comedy* as "the poem . . . that for many years hath kept me lean." He was intense in conviction, in action, and in the sufferings of his exile. He was intense in his faith in a God in whom power, wisdom, and love were fused in a radiance of supreme intensity.

Bergin, Thomas. *A Diversity of Dante*. New Brunswick, N.J.: Rutgers University Press, 1969.

A collection of essays on the work and life of

Dante, with much discussion of the art of narrative in the *Inferno*.

> It has always seemed to me that, like all good story tellers, Dante puts forth a great and calculated effort in the first chapter of his tale in order to seize our interest and give us the initial impetus to carry through. From the story-telling point of view, the *Inferno* is the richest of the three great divisions in action, variety, characterization, and dramatic description. Here, in the words of Malagoli, "poetry finds its place suspended, as it were, between the savor of concrete things and a breath of the sublime."

Musa, Mark. *Advent at the Gates: Dante's Comedy*. Bloomington: Indiana University Press, 1974.

A close literary study of Dante's attitudes to lust and political corruption. It points out that Dante, as an author, condemns the beautiful Francesca of *Inferno* Canto 5, while Dante as a literary character (pilgrim) is nearly seduced by her.

> But the more carefully we study the words of the courteous and cultivated Francesca, the more clearly we become aware of the flaws in her character which she is inadvertently revealing. Her basic weakness is her self-centeredness, and this can be seen even in her gracious attitude toward the Pilgrim.

Shapiro, Marianne. *Woman, Earthly and Divine, in the Comedy of Dante*. Lexington: University Press of Kentucky, 1975.

A study of Dante's complex view of women, on whom he cast responsibility for the Fall, but for whom he felt great admiration and love.

Most of the women who are mentioned or depicted as wives in the *Comedy* are sinful mainly in that they incite their husbands to sin. None of them are great sinners themselves. Few are more than one-dimensional. We know that Francesca's greatest sin is adultery and that Dido had a husband, but it is impossible to think of them as wives.

Foster, Kenelm. *The Two Dantes, and Other Studies*. Berkeley: University of California Press, 1977.
A study of the pagan and Christian polarities in Dante and his work.

In short, Dante's Hell is not only a picture of sin as it is (as one man saw it) but of sin as it would like to appear. . . . And the sin he encounters on his way is, I repeat, largely sin against the light of reason alone, apart from any "higher" considerations. It is wrongdoing very much on the human level and in the give and take of ordinary social intercourse.

1980s and Beyond

Holmes, George. *Dante*. New York: Oxford University Press, 1980.
A convenient, brief (104 pages) survey of the intent and shape of the *Comedy* and of its place in Dante's work as a whole.

Although the allegorical element is important and pervasive, one of the most striking and novel features of the *Comedy*, particularly of *Inferno*, is a certain kind of personal realism. Many of Dante's characters are, of course, legendary or historical figures of antiquity. But many others are people whom Dante knew or figures of the recent past whose characteristics were well known to him and to his contemporaries.

Kirkpatrick, Robin. *Dante, The Divine Comedy*. Cambridge, England: Cambridge University Press, 1987.

A brief but penetrating reading of the three books of the *Comedy*. It focuses on Dante's moral stance and the *Comedy*'s translation into narrative.

Plainly Dante himself was concerned in his poem with what he thought was true. Any fiction may claim a certain imaginative authenticity—but the *Comedy* is devoted to truth in the strongest sense. On Dante's account, his visionary journey is a privilege granted by a God who desires the human creature to know and understand the universe in which He has located it. The project rests upon a mystic confidence that God will finally allow the human being to "fix the gaze upon the eternal light" of truth (*Par*. XXXIII, 83). At the same time, the language in which Dante communicates the truth is—to an extent unexampled in subsequent literature—the language of exact science and logical demonstration.

Jacoff, Rachel, and William Stephany. *Inferno II*. Philadelphia: University of Pennsylvania Press, 1989.

One volume in the important series *Lectura Dantis Americana*, a collection of American scholarship on Dante, featuring close readings of Dante's texts. This volume gives a new translation of the second canto of the *Inferno* and offers several searching essays on its meaning.

> In *Inferno* II, Dante introduces his readers to what will become one of the *Commedia*'s central strategies: he begins here to establish his identity both as character and as author, by implicit comparison and contrast with other figures. Throughout the poem, each lover and each poet will shed light on Dante, as will each politician and each statesman, and especially each convert, the figures incrementally creating Dante's simultaneously unique and exemplary self-portrait. In *Inferno* II Dante begins this process, but not, as subsequently, through dialectical interchange with characters whom he encounters.

Mazzotta, Giuseppe. *Dante's Vision and the Circle of Knowledge*. Princeton, N.J.: Princeton University Press, 1993.

An authoritative and readable study of Dante's use of the learning of his time, for the *Inferno* as well as for the rest of the *Commedia*. A key book for understanding how and why Dante thought as he did.

> That Dante is a poet of justice hardly needs belaboring. But he is also a peace poet, and this needs a gloss. The tradition of peace poetry in Western literature is, to be sure, fairly skimpy. Poets—think of Bertran de Born, of Ezra Pound, of Dante himself in

his *De Vulgari Eloquentia*—would rather write of a call to arms and theorize a poetics of war. (In our age think of Hemingway; at most they write of a farewell to arms.) More often than not, they celebrate victories or they dream of peace as an escape from the savagery of war. They rarely write of peace as the condition for life and the aim of life, and almost never, if one excepts Tolstoy, Isaiah and the Gospels, of peace as a scandalous reproach to the ways of the world. Dante belongs to this tradition of scandal.

Cook, Albert. "Dante: Trasumanar per verba." In *The Reach of Poetry.* West Lafayette, Ind.: Purdue University Press, 1995.

Cook, one of the most brilliant critics of the Western literary tradition, scrutinizes the gamut of Dante's distinctive traits, from the terza rima verse form to the theological directness of the *Comedy.*

The encounters that release the *Divina Commedia* from the enclosedness of such poems ("Adam lay ibounden") and open it up for its ongoing expansions are with people we never meet in the world, thus providing the seal of fiction to the representation: the poet encounters real persons who lack an unpredictable future. They are complete because they are dead, and they are endowed by the poet with just what the dead lack, a communicative power to engage in a kind of dialogue.

Howard, Lloyd. *Formulas of Repetition in Dante's Commedia: Signposted Journeys Across Textual Space,* Montreal: Concordia University Press, 2002.

Studies the patterns of formulaic language and event in the *Commedia*.

Virgil descended before Christ, by journeying from Limbo to the very bottom of Hell. Essentially this was so that one individual, Dante, could descend and then ascend, just as Christ descended and ascended to show the way for all humankind to descend and then ascend toward salvation.

QUESTIONS FOR DISCUSSION

Do you think Hell is real? If you do, do you think it is a physical place? How does your vision of Hell compare to the Hell that Dante describes?

Is Dante's *Inferno* a fantasy? An allegory? A true inquiry into the way things are? Does Dante believe in a Hell of the kind he is writing about?

Why does Dante choose Virgil as his guide?

What insight into today's world can you gain from considering the fate of Mohammed in Hell? How does Dante's vision for Mohammed figure into the long history of Christian-Muslim antagonism and misunderstanding?

How does our contemporary ranking of sins or vices compare to Dante's? Dante was very hard on gluttony. Do we still consider it a sin? Would treachery to benefactors still rank as the supreme sin? And what about simony, or the sale of church offices, which is so offensive to Dante? Have we any equivalent to this sin? If you had to create nine circles of Hell, as Dante did, what kind of sinners would be in the first circle? What kind in the ninth?

What do you think of the consignment of Paolo and Francesca to Hell? (Canto V.) Does their adulterous sin seem to you to merit an eternity of being blown back and forth in the winds of Hell?

Recently, we've seen a revival of fantasy in films and literature. How do contemporary fantasy worlds like those presented in the *Lord of the Rings* trilogy compare to Dante's theological vision? What do they mean to us, compared to what the *Inferno* may have meant to its first readers?

SUGGESTIONS FOR THE INTERESTED READER

If you enjoyed *The Inferno*, you might also be interested in the following:

The Dante Club: A Novel, by Matthew Pearl. In this 2003 mystery-thriller, a team of nineteenth-century luminaries (including Henry Wadsworth Longfellow, Oliver Wendell Holmes, and James Russell Lowell) decide to spite the fusty scholars at Harvard who insist that Latin and Greek are the only true studies by bringing out a new American translation of Dante. However, before they can get their work truly under way, they are forced to hunt for a murderer who is terrorizing Boston by re-creating some of the most harrowing scenes from Dante's *Inferno*.

A TV Dante (VHS). Movie director Peter Greenaway (*Prospero's Books*) collaborated with book-art expert and Dante translator Tom Phillips to produce this 1989 made-for-British-TV version of the first eight cantos of the *Inferno*. It follows Phillips's translation exactly, interspersing actors reading the lines, talking-head style, with clips of more graphic representations.

No Exit, by Jean-Paul Sartre. This 1943 one-act existentialist play presents a modern vision of Hell very different from Dante's. The play is famous for its oft-quoted line: *"L'enfer, c'est les autres,"* meaning "Hell is other people."

The Name of the Rose, by Umberto Eco. A mystery novel set inside a monastery in 1327, this 1983 book features plenty of the tension between church and state with which Dante had to contend. A film version of the novel, starring Sean Connery and Christian Slater, was released in 1986.

The Lord of the Rings, by J.R.R. Tolkien. Tolkien's trilogy (published 1954–55), now the fabulously popular movie trilogy of the same name, traces the gentle Hobbit Frodo's journey into the hellish realm of Mordor and back. Tolkien was a professor of medieval literature in addition to being a writer, and while some of the cosmologies he draws from are very different, the works are structurally similar and make for a very interesting comparison.

Not sure what to read next?

Visit Pocket Books online at

www.SimonSays.com

Reading suggestions for
you and your reading group

New release news

Author appearances

Online chats with your favorite writers

Special offers

And much, much more!

10421